Mobile VPNs, Encryption, and Secure Browsing

How to Use VPNs, Encryption Tools, and Privacy Apps to Protect Your Mobile Internet Activity

By Joe Correa

Published by Live Stronger Faster

First Edition

Table of Contents

Introduction

Welcome to Mobile VPNs, Encryption, and Secure Browsing: How to Use VPNs, Encryption Tools, and Privacy Apps to Protect Your Mobile Internet Activity. This book is part of the Mobile Security & App Protection Academy: The Complete 10-in-1 Cybersecurity Collection, a comprehensive series designed to help everyday smartphone users, professionals, students, parents, business owners, and technology enthusiasts secure their mobile devices against modern digital threats. In this volume, we focus on one of the most important and often misunderstood aspects of mobile cybersecurity: protecting your internet activity, communications, and personal information from unwanted surveillance, cybercriminals, advertisers, data brokers, and other privacy threats.

Most people carry a smartphone everywhere they go. These devices have become digital wallets, communication centers, entertainment systems, navigation tools, personal assistants, and gateways to our financial accounts. Smartphones contain photographs, conversations, passwords, banking information, health records, business communications, personal contacts, and countless pieces of sensitive information that can reveal nearly every aspect of a person's life. While smartphones have become more powerful and convenient than ever before, they have also become valuable targets for cybercriminals and organizations seeking to collect user data.

Many people assume that using a smartphone automatically provides a certain level of security. Modern mobile operating systems such as Android and iOS do include many built-in security protections. However, even the most secure device can expose sensitive information when connected to insecure networks, poorly configured websites, untrusted applications, or online services that collect excessive amounts of personal data. The reality is that much of your privacy and security depends not only on your device but also on how your internet traffic travels across networks and how your data is protected while it is being transmitted.

Every time you connect your smartphone to the internet, your data passes through multiple systems before reaching its destination. Whether you are checking email, sending messages, accessing social media, watching videos, making purchases, or logging into a banking application, information is constantly moving between your device and remote servers. During this process, various parties may be able to observe, monitor, collect, or analyze portions of your activity. Internet service providers, public Wi-Fi operators, advertisers, data analytics companies, malicious hackers, and even certain applications may gather information about your browsing habits, location, interests, and online behavior.

Fortunately, powerful technologies exist to help protect your privacy and security. Virtual Private Networks (VPNs), encryption technologies, secure browsers, privacy-focused search engines, encrypted messaging applications, and other security tools can significantly reduce the amount of information exposed to third parties. When properly understood and used, these technologies create layers of protection that help safeguard your personal information while improving your overall cybersecurity posture.

One of the primary goals of this book is to eliminate confusion surrounding VPNs and encryption. These terms are often discussed in cybersecurity articles, advertisements, and technology forums, but many people do not fully understand what they do or how they work. Some users assume a VPN makes them completely anonymous online. Others believe encryption protects them from every possible cyber threat. While these technologies are powerful, they are not magic solutions. Understanding both their capabilities and limitations is essential for building realistic and effective security practices.

Throughout this book, you will learn how VPNs function, how encrypted connections protect your data, how secure browsing technologies work, and how to choose tools that align with your security needs. You will discover how internet traffic travels across networks, what information may be exposed during transmission, and how encryption helps prevent unauthorized access to sensitive communications. You will also learn how cybercriminals exploit insecure connections and how proper security configurations can help defend against common attacks.

Public Wi-Fi networks are one of the most common environments where mobile users face increased risk. Airports, hotels, coffee shops, restaurants, libraries, shopping centers, and public transportation hubs often provide convenient internet access. However, many users connect to these networks without understanding the potential dangers involved. Attackers may attempt to intercept network traffic, create fake Wi-Fi hotspots, monitor user activity, or exploit vulnerabilities in poorly secured networks. Understanding how to protect yourself while using public Wi-Fi is a critical skill in today's connected world.

Another major topic covered in this book is data privacy. Modern digital ecosystems are heavily driven by data collection. Many applications, websites, and online services gather information about users for advertising, analytics, personalization, and commercial purposes. While some data collection is necessary for functionality, excessive tracking can create significant privacy concerns. Many users are unaware of how much information is collected through browsing activity, app usage, location services, and online interactions. This book will help you understand how tracking systems operate and how privacy-focused tools can reduce unnecessary exposure.

Encryption serves as the foundation of modern digital security. Without encryption, sensitive information such as passwords, financial transactions, medical records, and private communications could be easily intercepted and read by unauthorized parties. Encryption transforms readable data into encoded information that can only be accessed by authorized users possessing the correct decryption keys. While the technical details behind encryption can be complex, this book explains the concepts in practical, easy-to-understand language that focuses on real-world application rather than mathematical theory.

Secure communication is another area where encryption plays a vital role. Messaging applications, email services, cloud storage platforms, and collaboration tools increasingly rely on encryption to protect user data. However, not all services provide the same level of protection. Some services encrypt data only during transmission, while others offer end-to-end encryption that prevents even the service provider from accessing message content. Understanding these differences allows users to make informed decisions about which tools are appropriate for sensitive communications.

Privacy-focused browsing is becoming increasingly important as online tracking technologies grow more sophisticated. Websites may use cookies, browser fingerprinting techniques, advertising trackers, analytics tools, and other mechanisms to monitor user behavior across the internet. While some tracking supports useful functionality, excessive tracking can create detailed profiles of users' interests, habits, and activities. This book will explore how privacy-oriented browsers, search engines, browser settings, and protective tools can help reduce unwanted tracking while maintaining a functional browsing experience.

You will also learn about mobile privacy applications that enhance security beyond traditional VPNs and browsers. These tools may include encrypted messaging platforms, password managers, secure email services, private cloud storage providers, DNS protection tools, and mobile security applications designed to improve privacy and reduce exposure to cyber threats. Together, these technologies create multiple layers of defense that strengthen your overall digital security strategy.

As mobile technology continues to evolve, so do the threats facing users. Cybercriminals constantly develop new methods for stealing information, monitoring communications, distributing malware, and exploiting user behavior. Security is not a one-time action but an ongoing process that requires awareness, education, and adaptation. By understanding how modern threats operate and how defensive technologies work, users can make better decisions and significantly reduce their risk.

The purpose of this book is not to create fear but to build confidence. Cybersecurity can sometimes appear intimidating due to technical terminology and rapidly changing threats. However, effective security often comes down to understanding a few core principles and consistently applying good habits. The tools discussed throughout this book are designed to empower users, giving them greater control over their privacy, security, and online experience.

Whether you are a beginner seeking to protect your personal information, a professional handling sensitive business data, a student using public networks, a traveler connecting through unfamiliar Wi-Fi systems, or simply someone who values privacy, the lessons contained in this book will provide practical knowledge that can be applied immediately. By the end of your journey through this volume, you will have a stronger understanding of VPNs, encryption technologies, secure browsing practices, privacy protection strategies, and the layered security approach necessary for navigating today's digital world safely and confidently.

The internet offers incredible opportunities for communication, education, commerce, creativity, and personal growth. At the same time, it presents risks that must be understood and managed. The goal is not to disconnect from technology but to use it wisely. Through knowledge, awareness, and proper security practices, you can enjoy the benefits of mobile connectivity while maintaining greater control over your personal information and digital identity. Let us begin the journey toward stronger mobile privacy, safer internet activity, and a more secure digital future.

Chapter 1

Comprehending Mobile Privacy, VPNs, and Secure Internet Connections

The modern smartphone has become one of the most important devices in daily life. Most people use their phones to communicate with family and friends, access financial accounts, shop online, manage business operations, store personal photographs, navigate unfamiliar locations, and consume information from around the world. While these conveniences have transformed society, they have also created new privacy and security challenges. Every time a smartphone connects to the internet, information is exchanged between the device and various servers, networks, applications, and services. Understanding how this information travels and how it can be protected is the foundation of mobile privacy and cybersecurity.

Many users mistakenly believe that internet activity is private by default. In reality, a considerable amount of information may be visible to internet service providers, network operators, websites, applications, advertisers, and potentially cybercriminals if proper protections are not in place. Mobile devices constantly transmit data including location information, browsing requests, app activity, device identifiers, and communication traffic. While much of this activity is necessary for functionality, users should understand what information is being shared and how to control their digital footprint.

To understand mobile privacy, it is important to first understand how internet communication works. When a user enters a website address or opens an application, the device sends requests through the internet to remote servers. These requests travel through multiple systems before reaching their destination. During this journey, data may pass through local Wi-Fi networks, internet service providers, regional network hubs, and various routing systems. Without adequate protection, portions of this communication may be observed or analyzed by unauthorized parties.

One of the most significant risks occurs when users connect to public Wi-Fi networks. Public networks are commonly found in airports, hotels, restaurants, shopping centers, libraries, and coffee shops. While convenient, these networks often present greater security risks than trusted home or business networks. Cybercriminals may create fake Wi-Fi hotspots designed to imitate legitimate networks. Unsuspecting users connect to these fake networks and unknowingly expose their internet traffic to attackers. In other cases, poorly secured public networks may allow malicious individuals to monitor unencrypted traffic.

This is where Virtual Private Networks, commonly known as VPNs, become valuable security tools. A VPN creates an encrypted tunnel between the user's device and a secure server operated by the VPN provider. Rather than sending internet traffic directly through the local network, the VPN encrypts the data before it leaves the device. This encryption makes it significantly more difficult for others to intercept or analyze the information being transmitted.

When using a VPN, internet traffic first travels to the VPN server before reaching its final destination. Websites and online services typically see the VPN server's address rather than the user's actual network address. This process helps improve privacy by reducing direct exposure of the user's internet connection details. It also protects data traveling across potentially insecure networks by encrypting communications during transit.

However, understanding the limitations of VPN technology is just as important as understanding its benefits. A VPN does not make users invisible online. It does not eliminate malware infections, prevent phishing attacks, or guarantee complete anonymity. If a user voluntarily provides personal information to a website, falls victim to a scam, or downloads malicious software, a VPN alone cannot prevent those actions. Effective security requires multiple layers of protection working together.

Encryption serves as the foundation of VPN technology and modern internet security. Encryption converts readable information into coded data that can only be interpreted by authorized parties possessing the appropriate decryption keys. Imagine sending a message in a locked container that only the intended recipient can open. Even if someone intercepts the container during transit, they cannot easily access its contents without the key. This concept forms the basis of digital encryption.

Encryption protects sensitive information such as passwords, financial transactions, medical records, private messages, and login credentials. Modern encryption algorithms are designed to withstand sophisticated attacks and provide strong protection against unauthorized access. While no system is completely invulnerable, properly implemented encryption significantly reduces the risk of data exposure.

Another important aspect of mobile privacy involves understanding metadata. Many users focus only on the content of their communications while overlooking metadata.

Metadata includes information about who communicated, when communication occurred, how long it lasted, device information, geographic location, and network details. Even when message content is encrypted, metadata may still reveal significant information about user behavior and patterns. Privacy-conscious users should understand that protecting privacy often involves minimizing unnecessary data collection rather than focusing solely on message content.

Mobile applications represent another major source of privacy exposure. Many apps request access to permissions such as location services, contacts, microphone access, camera functionality, storage, and device information. While some permissions are necessary for app functionality, others may collect more information than users realize. Understanding application permissions and regularly reviewing access settings can significantly improve mobile privacy.

Users should develop the habit of evaluating whether requested permissions are reasonable. A navigation app may legitimately require location access, but a simple flashlight application generally does not need access to contacts, microphone data, or photo libraries. By limiting unnecessary permissions, users reduce the amount of information available to third parties and decrease potential attack surfaces.

Secure browsing practices also play an essential role in mobile cybersecurity. Modern web browsers include various security features designed to protect users from malicious websites, tracking systems, and harmful downloads. Keeping browsers updated ensures that security vulnerabilities are patched promptly. Outdated software often becomes a target for cybercriminals seeking to exploit known weaknesses.

HTTPS technology is another critical component of secure browsing. Websites using HTTPS encrypt communications between the user's browser and the website server. This protection helps prevent attackers from intercepting sensitive information such as passwords, login credentials, and payment information. Users should verify that websites handling sensitive data utilize secure HTTPS connections before submitting personal information.

Privacy-focused search engines can further reduce unnecessary data collection. Traditional search engines often collect extensive information about search history, user interests, device information, and browsing behavior. Privacy-oriented alternatives seek to minimize data retention and reduce user profiling. While no solution provides perfect privacy, these tools can help limit exposure to large-scale tracking systems.

Another common misconception is that privacy and convenience cannot coexist. While stronger privacy protections may require minor adjustments, many security tools are designed to operate seamlessly in the background. VPNs, encrypted messaging apps, secure browsers, and password managers often function with minimal impact on daily activities while providing substantial security benefits.

Password management deserves special attention within any mobile security strategy. Weak or reused passwords remain one of the most common causes of account compromise. Password managers generate and store strong, unique passwords for multiple accounts while protecting them through encryption. This approach reduces the risk associated with password reuse and simplifies credential management.

Multi-factor authentication provides an additional layer of protection beyond passwords. Even if an attacker obtains a user's password, multi-factor authentication requires a second verification factor before granting account access. This additional step significantly reduces the likelihood of unauthorized account compromise and should be enabled whenever available.

Ultimately, mobile privacy is not achieved through a single tool or application. Instead, it results from combining multiple protective measures that work together. VPNs protect internet traffic. Encryption secures sensitive data. Secure browsers reduce exposure to malicious websites. Privacy-focused applications limit tracking. Strong passwords and multi-factor authentication protect accounts. Together, these layers create a comprehensive security strategy that reduces risk while maintaining usability.

As cyber threats continue to evolve, users who understand these foundational principles will be better prepared to protect themselves. The remainder of this book will build upon these concepts, providing practical guidance for selecting VPN services, implementing encryption tools, improving browsing privacy, and creating a mobile security environment that supports both convenience and protection.

Michael installed a reputable VPN service

Michael considered himself reasonably careful online. He used a smartphone for nearly everything, including banking, shopping, communicating with clients, and managing family activities. Yet he rarely thought about how his information traveled across the internet. Like many people, he assumed that modern technology automatically provided sufficient security.

One morning, while waiting for a flight at a busy airport, Michael connected to a public Wi-Fi network called "Airport Free WiFi." The network appeared legitimate, and connecting allowed him to save mobile data while catching up on emails. He logged into several accounts, checked his bank balance, responded to business messages, and made travel arrangements without giving the situation much thought.

A few days later, Michael noticed unusual activity on one of his online accounts. An unfamiliar login alert appeared from a location he had never visited. Initially, he assumed it was an error, but additional alerts soon followed. Concerned, he changed his password and began investigating what might have happened.

Michael contacted a cybersecurity consultant named Sarah, who specialized in helping individuals improve their digital security. During their conversation, Sarah asked detailed questions about recent online activity, travel, networks used, and account access patterns. When Michael mentioned the airport Wi-Fi connection, Sarah immediately became interested.

She explained that public Wi-Fi networks can present significant risks. Some attackers create fake networks that closely resemble legitimate hotspots. Unsuspecting users connect and unknowingly route their internet traffic through systems controlled by cybercriminals. Even legitimate public networks can present risks if users transmit sensitive information without adequate protection.

Michael was surprised. He had assumed that because the network appeared professional and widely used, it was safe. Sarah explained that appearance alone does not guarantee security. Attackers often exploit trust and convenience rather than relying solely on technical sophistication.

Over the following weeks, Sarah guided Michael through a complete mobile privacy assessment. They reviewed installed applications, browser settings, account security measures, password practices, and network habits. The results were eye-opening. Several applications possessed unnecessary permissions. Multiple accounts used similar passwords. Location tracking was enabled for apps that had no legitimate need for it.

Together, they implemented improvements. Michael installed a reputable VPN service and learned how it protected his internet traffic, particularly when using public networks. He enabled multi-factor authentication on important accounts. He adopted a password manager that generated strong, unique credentials for every service he used. He also began reviewing app permissions regularly.

At first, Michael worried that these changes would complicate daily life. Instead, he discovered that most security tools operated quietly in the background. The VPN connected automatically when joining unfamiliar networks. The password manager simplified logins. Multi-factor authentication added only a few seconds to account access while dramatically improving security.

Several months later, Michael found himself once again sitting in an airport waiting for a delayed flight. This time, however, his perspective had changed. As he connected to the airport Wi-Fi, his VPN automatically activated. He felt confident knowing that his internet traffic was encrypted before leaving his device.

Nearby, he overheard another traveler discussing concerns about online privacy and public Wi-Fi risks. Michael found himself explaining many of the same concepts Sarah had taught him. He described how VPNs worked, why encryption mattered, and how simple habits could significantly improve digital security.

The traveler listened carefully and admitted that he had never considered most of those issues. Michael smiled because he remembered feeling exactly the same way only months earlier. The difference was education. Once he understood how mobile networks, privacy risks, and security tools functioned, protecting himself became much easier.

As his knowledge grew, Michael became more aware of how often personal information moved across digital systems. Rather than creating fear, this awareness gave him confidence. He no longer relied solely on assumptions. He understood the tools available to him and knew how to use them effectively.

By the end of the year, Michael's online habits had transformed completely. Security was no longer an afterthought but a routine part of daily life. He used secure networks whenever possible, relied on encryption technologies, monitored account activity, and remained cautious when granting application permissions. Most importantly, he understood that privacy and security were ongoing processes rather than one-time solutions.

The lessons Michael learned reflected a truth that applies to every smartphone user. Mobile security begins with awareness. Understanding how information travels, where risks exist, and which tools provide protection empowers individuals to take control of their digital lives. While technology will continue to evolve, the principles of privacy, encryption, and secure communication remain essential foundations for safe and confident mobile internet use.

Chapter 2

How VPNs Work and Choosing the Right Mobile VPN

Virtual Private Networks, commonly known as VPNs, have become one of the most widely recommended tools for improving online privacy and security. While many people have heard the term VPN through advertisements, social media promotions, technology blogs, or cybersecurity discussions, relatively few users fully understand how VPN technology works behind the scenes. This chapter will explain the core concepts of VPN functionality, the advantages and limitations of VPN services, and how to choose the right VPN solution for mobile devices.

To understand VPNs, it is helpful to first examine what normally happens when a smartphone connects to the internet. Under standard circumstances, internet traffic travels from the user's device through a local network and then through the user's internet service provider before reaching websites, applications, and online services. During this process, various parties may be able to observe certain information about the connection. Depending on the situation, this could include network operators, internet providers, advertisers, or potentially cybercriminals monitoring insecure networks.

When a VPN is activated, the process changes significantly. Instead of sending internet traffic directly to its destination, the smartphone first establishes a secure encrypted connection with a VPN server. This encrypted connection is often referred to as a tunnel because it creates a protected pathway through which data travels. Once traffic reaches the VPN server, it is then forwarded to the intended destination. Responses from websites and online services travel back through the VPN server and return to the user's device through the encrypted tunnel.

One of the primary benefits of this approach is that anyone monitoring the local network can see that encrypted data is being transmitted but cannot easily determine the specific contents of that traffic. This protection becomes particularly valuable when using public Wi-Fi networks in locations such as airports, hotels, restaurants, libraries, convention centers, and coffee shops. Public networks may expose users to increased risk because they are often shared by many individuals and may not be properly secured.

The encryption used by modern VPN services helps protect data from interception while it travels across networks.

Encryption transforms readable information into coded data that can only be deciphered by authorized systems possessing the correct cryptographic keys. Without encryption, attackers who successfully intercept traffic may be able to view sensitive information such as login credentials, messages, financial transactions, or browsing activity. Encryption significantly reduces this risk.

Another important feature of VPN technology involves IP address masking. Every internet-connected device uses an IP address that helps route communications across networks. Websites and online services often see the IP address associated with the user's internet connection. When using a VPN, websites generally see the IP address of the VPN server rather than the user's original network address. This process adds a layer of privacy by making it more difficult for websites to directly associate activity with a user's physical internet connection.

Many VPN providers operate server networks across multiple countries and regions. Users can often choose which server location they wish to use. For example, a person physically located in one country may connect through a VPN server located in another country. While this capability is sometimes used to access region-specific content, it also provides flexibility for users seeking additional privacy or secure connectivity while traveling internationally.

Understanding VPN protocols is also important when evaluating VPN services. A VPN protocol refers to the set of rules governing how data is encrypted and transmitted between the device and VPN server. Modern VPN providers commonly support protocols such as OpenVPN, WireGuard, and IKEv2/IPsec. Each protocol offers different advantages regarding speed, security, efficiency, and compatibility. While most users do not need to understand every technical detail, selecting providers that utilize modern, well-regarded protocols contributes to stronger security.

WireGuard has gained popularity due to its combination of speed, simplicity, and strong security architecture. OpenVPN remains widely respected because of its long history, extensive security audits, and broad compatibility. IKEv2/IPsec is often valued for its stability on mobile devices and its ability to maintain connections during network transitions, such as moving between Wi-Fi and cellular networks.

Many VPN providers advertise strict no-logs policies. This term refers to how much user activity data the provider stores. A true no-logs policy means the provider does not retain records of browsing activity, connection histories, or other identifying information that could be linked to individual users. However, not all no-logs claims are equal. Responsible users should examine whether a provider's policies have been independently audited and whether the company operates in a jurisdiction with strong privacy protections.

Transparency is an important factor when selecting a VPN provider. Reputable providers clearly explain their privacy practices, security features, ownership structure, and legal obligations. Companies that provide independent audit reports, open-source software components, and detailed privacy documentation often demonstrate a stronger commitment to user trust than providers making vague marketing claims.

Free VPN services deserve special consideration. While some legitimate free VPN options exist, many free services generate revenue through advertising, data collection, bandwidth limitations, or premium subscription upselling. Because operating VPN infrastructure requires significant resources, users should carefully evaluate how a free service sustains its business operations. If a provider offers extensive services without clear revenue sources, users should investigate whether data collection practices may be involved.

Performance is another important consideration. VPNs introduce additional steps into internet communications because traffic must travel through the VPN server before reaching its destination. This process may affect connection speed, latency, or battery consumption. Modern VPN providers work to minimize these impacts through optimized infrastructure and efficient protocols. Users should seek providers with reliable performance and server availability in regions relevant to their needs.

Mobile VPN applications often include additional security features beyond basic encryption. Some providers offer kill switches that automatically block internet access if the VPN connection unexpectedly disconnects. This feature prevents traffic from accidentally being transmitted through an unprotected connection. Other providers include DNS leak protection, malware filtering, tracker blocking, ad blocking, or secure browsing enhancements.

DNS protection is particularly valuable because DNS requests translate website names into numerical addresses used by computers. Without proper protection, DNS requests may reveal browsing activity even when other traffic is encrypted. High-quality VPN services often include secure DNS handling to reduce information leakage.

Users should also understand situations where VPN protection may be limited. A VPN encrypts traffic between the device and VPN server, but it cannot protect information that users voluntarily provide to websites, applications, or online services. Logging into social media accounts, submitting personal forms, or sharing information through unsecured services may still expose personal data regardless of VPN usage.

Similarly, VPNs do not replace antivirus software, mobile security tools, software updates, strong passwords, or safe browsing practices. Effective cybersecurity requires multiple layers of protection working together. A VPN represents one important component within a broader security strategy rather than a complete solution by itself.

For business users, VPNs can play an especially important role. Employees who access company systems remotely often use VPN connections to securely transmit sensitive business information. Mobile professionals frequently connect through airports, hotels, client locations, and public networks where secure communications are essential. VPN technology helps reduce risk while supporting productivity and mobility.

Travelers also benefit significantly from VPN protection. International travel may expose users to unfamiliar network environments, varying privacy regulations, and increased surveillance risks. A trusted VPN can provide consistent protection regardless of location, helping maintain privacy and security while away from home.

When selecting a mobile VPN, users should evaluate several key factors: security protocols, privacy policies, independent audits, company reputation, server availability, application usability, customer support, performance, and pricing. Choosing a trustworthy provider may require some research, but the effort is worthwhile given the sensitive role VPNs play in protecting internet activity.

Ultimately, VPNs provide valuable protection by encrypting internet traffic, reducing exposure on public networks, improving privacy, and helping users maintain greater control over their digital activities. Understanding how VPNs function and selecting reputable providers empowers users to make informed decisions that strengthen their overall mobile cybersecurity posture.

David attended a cybersecurity presentation

David traveled frequently for his consulting business. Nearly every week involved airports, hotels, client offices, conference centers, and unfamiliar cities. His smartphone served as his primary communication tool, allowing him to manage projects, review documents, attend virtual meetings, and stay connected with clients while on the move.

For years, David paid little attention to internet security. He connected to any available Wi-Fi network without hesitation and assumed that modern technology automatically protected his information. His focus remained on convenience rather than security.

One afternoon during a business conference, David attended a cybersecurity presentation led by an expert named Rebecca. The session focused on protecting mobile devices during travel. Rebecca discussed public Wi-Fi risks, encrypted communications, VPN technology, and common misconceptions about online privacy.

David was surprised by many of the examples she presented. He learned how attackers sometimes created fake wireless networks that mimicked legitimate hotspots. He learned that public networks often provided opportunities for monitoring unprotected traffic. Most importantly, he learned that many travelers exposed sensitive business information without realizing it.

After the presentation, David approached Rebecca and asked for practical advice. He explained that he spent much of his time working from airports, hotels, and conference venues.

Rebecca recommended that he begin using a reputable VPN service and explained how encrypted tunnels protected internet traffic while traveling.

Curious, David spent the following weekend researching VPN providers. Initially, he felt overwhelmed by the number of options available. Every provider claimed to be the fastest, most secure, and most private. Marketing language filled websites with promises of complete anonymity and perfect protection.

Remembering Rebecca's advice, David focused on substance rather than advertising. He examined privacy policies, reviewed independent audits, studied security protocols, and read technical evaluations from trusted cybersecurity sources. Eventually, he selected a provider with a strong reputation, transparent policies, and modern encryption standards.

Installing the VPN on his smartphone proved surprisingly simple. Within minutes, the application was configured and operational. The interface allowed him to select server locations, enable automatic protection on public networks, and activate security features such as a kill switch and DNS protection.

During his next business trip, David noticed an immediate difference in his mindset. While waiting for a connecting flight, he connected to airport Wi-Fi. Instead of feeling uncertain about the security of the network, he knew that his VPN encrypted traffic before it left his device. Emails, documents, messages, and business communications traveled through a protected tunnel.

Over the next several months, the VPN became part of his daily routine. The application automatically activated whenever he joined unfamiliar networks. He rarely needed to think about it because the protection operated quietly in the background.

One evening, David met another consultant named Mark at a hotel lounge. As they discussed technology and travel, Mark mentioned concerns about privacy while working remotely. David shared what he had learned about VPNs and encrypted communications.

Mark admitted that he had heard of VPNs but assumed they were only useful for technology professionals. David explained that the tools were actually designed for ordinary users. He described how encryption protected internet traffic and how modern VPN applications simplified security without requiring technical expertise.

Their conversation continued for nearly an hour. David realized how much his understanding had evolved since attending Rebecca's presentation. Concepts that once seemed confusing now felt straightforward because he had taken the time to learn the fundamentals.

Several weeks later, David experienced a situation that reinforced the value of his new habits. While attending a conference overseas, he noticed multiple Wi-Fi networks with nearly identical names. Conference staff later announced that attackers had created fake networks to lure attendees into connecting.

Many participants panicked when they learned of the incident. David remained calm. Although he could not guarantee complete protection, he knew that his VPN encrypted traffic during the event. Combined with strong passwords and multi-factor authentication, his security measures significantly reduced potential exposure.

That experience changed how he viewed cybersecurity. He no longer considered security tools unnecessary inconveniences. Instead, he saw them as practical safeguards that reduced risk while supporting his professional activities.

Months later, Rebecca invited David to speak briefly during another cybersecurity workshop. Rather than presenting technical details, he shared his personal journey. He described how little he had understood about mobile privacy, how easily public networks could expose users to risk, and how simple tools like VPNs had improved his security.

The audience responded positively because many attendees saw themselves in David's story. They were busy professionals, travelers, students, and everyday smartphone users seeking practical solutions rather than complicated technical explanations.

As the workshop concluded, David reflected on the lesson he had learned. Effective security did not require becoming a cybersecurity expert. It required understanding basic risks, choosing trustworthy tools, and developing consistent habits. VPN technology represented one of those habits—a simple yet powerful layer of protection that helped secure internet activity wherever life and work took him.

His experience demonstrated an important truth. Knowledge transforms security from something intimidating into something manageable. Once users understand how VPNs function and how to choose reliable providers, they gain the confidence needed to protect themselves in an increasingly connected world.

public networks could expose users to risk, and how simple tools like VPNs had improved his security.

The audience responded positively because many saw themselves in David's story. They were busy professionals, travelers, students, and everyday smartphone users seeking practical solutions rather than complicated technical explanations.

As the workshop concluded, David reflected on the lesson he had learned: effective security did not require becoming a cybersecurity expert. It required understanding basic risks, choosing trustworthy tools, and developing consistent habits. VPN technology represented one of those habits—a simple yet powerful layer of protection that helped secure internet activity across life and work.

The experience reinforced an important point: knowledge [illegible] When users understand how VPNs function and how to choose reliable providers, they gain the confidence needed to protect themselves in an increasingly connected world.

Chapter 3

Encryption Fundamentals for Mobile Devices and Communications

Encryption is one of the most important technologies in modern cybersecurity. Every day, billions of people rely on encryption without even realizing it. Whenever a person sends a secure message, logs into an online account, uses a banking application, makes an online purchase, accesses cloud storage, or communicates through many popular mobile apps, encryption is often working behind the scenes to protect sensitive information. Despite its widespread use, many people do not fully understand what encryption is, how it works, or why it is so essential to mobile security. Understanding the fundamentals of encryption allows users to make better decisions about protecting their personal information and maintaining privacy in a connected world.

At its most basic level, encryption is the process of converting readable information into an unreadable format that can only be accessed by authorized parties. Imagine writing a message using a secret code that only you and the intended recipient understand. Anyone intercepting the message would see symbols or meaningless text rather than the original information. Digital encryption operates on a similar principle, although it uses advanced mathematical algorithms rather than simple substitution codes.

The information that users can normally read is known as plaintext. When encryption is applied, the plaintext is transformed into ciphertext. Ciphertext appears as random data and cannot be understood without the appropriate decryption key. The decryption key is a specific piece of information that allows authorized users or systems to convert the ciphertext back into readable plaintext. Without the correct key, deciphering properly encrypted data becomes extremely difficult and often practically impossible with current computing capabilities.

Encryption serves several critical purposes in cybersecurity. First, it protects confidentiality by ensuring that unauthorized individuals cannot access sensitive information. Second, it supports data integrity by helping verify that information has not been altered during transmission. Third, it contributes to authentication by confirming that communications originate from trusted sources. Together, these benefits make encryption a cornerstone of modern digital security.

Mobile devices store enormous amounts of sensitive information. Smartphones often contain emails, photographs, videos, contacts, financial records, business documents, passwords, browsing histories, location data, health information, and personal communications. If a device is lost, stolen, or compromised, unencrypted data may become accessible to unauthorized individuals. Device encryption helps address this risk by protecting stored information and requiring authentication before data can be accessed.

Modern Android and iPhone devices typically include built-in encryption capabilities. When properly configured, these systems encrypt the contents of the device's storage. If someone physically obtains the device, the encrypted data remains inaccessible without the correct passcode, password, biometric authentication, or security credentials. This protection significantly reduces the likelihood of data exposure following theft or loss.

One of the most common forms of encryption encountered by users is transport encryption. Transport encryption protects data while it travels between devices and servers. When users access secure websites using HTTPS, encryption protects communications during transmission. This prevents attackers from easily intercepting passwords, financial information, personal messages, and other sensitive data while it moves across networks.

HTTPS stands for Hypertext Transfer Protocol Secure. It is the secure version of the protocol used to communicate between web browsers and websites. HTTPS relies on encryption technologies known as SSL or TLS. Modern systems primarily use TLS, which stands for Transport Layer Security. When users see a secure connection indicator in their browser, TLS encryption is helping protect communications from interception.

TLS works by establishing a secure session between the user's device and the website. During this process, the browser and server exchange information that allows them to create encrypted communications. Once the connection is established, information transmitted between the two systems is encrypted before being sent across the internet. This process occurs within seconds and usually remains invisible to the user.

Another important category of encryption is end-to-end encryption. End-to-end encryption provides stronger privacy protections because messages are encrypted on the sender's device and can only be decrypted on the recipient's device. Even the service provider facilitating communication cannot read the content of properly encrypted messages. This approach is commonly used by secure messaging applications that prioritize user privacy.

The distinction between transport encryption and end-to-end encryption is important. Transport encryption protects data while it travels between systems, but service providers may still access the information once it reaches their servers. End-to-end encryption extends protection by ensuring that only the communicating parties can access message contents. Users handling highly sensitive information should understand which applications provide end-to-end encryption and under what circumstances.

Encryption relies heavily on cryptographic keys. These keys function like highly sophisticated digital passwords used by mathematical algorithms to encrypt and decrypt data. The strength of encryption often depends on key length, algorithm design, implementation quality, and key management practices. Even the strongest encryption can be undermined if keys are poorly protected or improperly handled.

Two major categories of encryption exist: symmetric encryption and asymmetric encryption. Symmetric encryption uses a single key for both encryption and decryption. This method is generally fast and efficient, making it suitable for encrypting large amounts of data. However, it requires a secure method of sharing the encryption key between authorized parties.

Asymmetric encryption uses two related keys: a public key and a private key. The public key can be shared openly, while the private key remains secret. Information encrypted with the public key can only be decrypted using the corresponding private key. This approach helps solve key distribution challenges and plays a vital role in secure internet communications, digital certificates, and authentication systems.

Digital certificates represent another important component of modern encryption systems. Certificates help verify the identity of websites, applications, and servers. When a user visits a secure website, the browser examines the site's certificate to confirm that it belongs to the expected organization. This process helps protect users from fraudulent websites attempting to impersonate legitimate services.

Despite the strength of encryption technologies, users should recognize that encryption is not a complete security solution. Encrypted systems can still be compromised through phishing attacks, social engineering, malware infections, weak passwords, or poor security practices. For example, if a cybercriminal tricks a user into revealing login credentials, encryption may not prevent unauthorized account access.

Strong authentication remains essential. Multi-factor authentication adds additional layers of protection by requiring multiple forms of verification before granting access to accounts or systems. Combining encryption with strong authentication significantly improves overall security and reduces the likelihood of unauthorized access.

Cloud storage services frequently use encryption to protect user data. However, encryption practices vary among providers. Some services encrypt data during transmission and storage while retaining access to decryption keys. Others offer zero-knowledge architectures where only the user controls the encryption keys. Understanding these differences allows users to make informed decisions about where sensitive information is stored.

Encrypted backups are equally important. Mobile devices can fail, become damaged, or be stolen. Secure backups ensure that information remains recoverable while protecting it from unauthorized access. Users should verify that backup systems utilize strong encryption and secure authentication mechanisms.

Encryption also plays a crucial role in mobile payment systems. Digital wallets, banking applications, and payment processors use encryption to protect financial transactions and account information. These protections help secure sensitive data during purchases, transfers, and account management activities. Without encryption, modern digital commerce would be far more vulnerable to fraud and theft.

As technology evolves, encryption continues to adapt to emerging threats. Researchers constantly develop stronger algorithms, improved protocols, and more secure implementations. While no security technology is perfect, encryption remains one of the most effective tools available for protecting digital information.

For mobile users, understanding encryption fundamentals provides a valuable foundation for making informed security decisions. By enabling device encryption, using secure communications platforms, verifying HTTPS connections, protecting authentication credentials, and selecting privacy-conscious services, users can significantly improve their cybersecurity posture. Encryption may operate behind the scenes, but its role in safeguarding personal information is both powerful and indispensable.

Emily considered herself technologically capable

Emily worked as a financial consultant and spent much of her day communicating with clients through email, messaging applications, cloud platforms, and mobile banking systems.

Her smartphone functioned as a portable office, allowing her to review reports, conduct meetings, and manage sensitive information from virtually anywhere.

Although Emily considered herself technologically capable, she had never devoted much attention to encryption. Like many people, she viewed security as something handled automatically by technology companies. As long as her applications worked correctly, she rarely thought about the mechanisms protecting her data.

One afternoon, Emily attended a professional conference focused on digital business practices. During one session, a cybersecurity expert named Jonathan delivered a presentation about data protection and mobile security. He discussed encryption, secure communications, identity theft, and the increasing importance of protecting sensitive information.

Jonathan began with a simple question.

"If someone intercepted your messages, financial records, or client information today, what would they learn about you?"

The room became quiet.

Emily realized she had never seriously considered the possibility. Her phone contained years of emails, client communications, contracts, financial data, photographs, and personal conversations. The amount of information stored on a single device was staggering.

Jonathan explained how encryption protected that information. Using practical examples rather than technical jargon, he described how encrypted data became unreadable to unauthorized parties. He compared encryption to placing valuable documents inside an advanced digital vault that only authorized individuals could open.

The presentation sparked Emily's curiosity. After returning home, she began researching mobile encryption and reviewing her own security settings. What she discovered surprised her. While many protections were already enabled, several important security features remained underutilized.

She enabled stronger device security settings, reviewed backup configurations, and activated additional authentication protections on important accounts. She also examined the communication tools she used daily and learned which applications provided end-to-end encryption versus standard transport encryption.

Over the following weeks, Emily became increasingly aware of how often encryption protected her activities. Every secure website connection, banking transaction, cloud backup, and encrypted message relied on technologies she had previously taken for granted.

One day, a colleague named Robert approached her with concerns about mobile security. His smartphone had recently been stolen during a business trip, and he worried about the information stored on the device.

Emily shared what she had learned. She explained how device encryption could protect stored information even if a phone was physically stolen. She described the importance of strong passcodes and remote device management features. Most importantly, she emphasized that security should be planned before an incident occurs rather than afterward.

Fortunately, Robert had enabled device encryption before the theft. Security professionals later confirmed that the data remained protected because the phone's storage could not be accessed without proper authentication credentials.

The experience reinforced Emily's growing appreciation for encryption. She realized that effective security often involved invisible protections working quietly behind the scenes. Users rarely noticed encryption when everything functioned normally, yet its importance became immediately apparent during security incidents.

Several months later, Emily's company launched a project involving highly sensitive financial information. Management requested recommendations for secure communications and data protection practices. Because of her recent studies, Emily volunteered to assist.

Working alongside information security specialists, she helped evaluate communication platforms, storage systems, authentication controls, and encryption standards. The process deepened her understanding of how organizations rely on encryption to protect both business operations and customer trust.

One evening, while reviewing project documentation, Emily reflected on how much her perspective had changed. Before attending Jonathan's presentation, encryption seemed like an abstract technical concept reserved for cybersecurity professionals. Now she recognized it as a practical and essential component of everyday life.

Every secure purchase, confidential message, protected document, and verified login depended upon encryption technologies operating behind the scenes. These systems protected not only corporations and governments but also ordinary individuals conducting daily activities through their mobile devices.

Later that year, Emily encountered Jonathan again at another conference. She thanked him for inspiring her interest in mobile security and shared the positive changes she had implemented. Jonathan smiled and explained that education often creates the strongest security improvement of all.

Technology alone cannot solve every problem. However, informed users make better decisions. They recognize risks, understand available protections, and apply security measures consistently. Encryption becomes most effective when combined with awareness, good habits, and responsible digital behavior.

As Emily left the conference, she reflected on that lesson. Security was not about fear or paranoia. It was about understanding how technology worked and using that knowledge to protect valuable information. Encryption represented one of the most powerful tools available for achieving that goal.

From that point forward, she no longer viewed encryption as an invisible background process. She saw it as a trusted guardian working continuously to protect her communications, finances, personal information, and professional responsibilities. The technology itself remained largely unseen, but its value became unmistakably clear.

For Emily, understanding encryption transformed cybersecurity from a mysterious technical subject into a practical skill. And that knowledge gave her confidence as she navigated an increasingly connected digital world.

Chapter 4

Secure Browsing on Mobile Devices and Protecting Yourself from Online Tracking

Every time a person uses a smartphone to access the internet, a significant amount of information is exchanged between the device and websites, applications, advertising networks, analytics providers, and other digital services. Most users think of browsing as a simple activity involving reading articles, watching videos, shopping online, checking email, or using social media. However, behind the scenes, complex systems are constantly collecting, processing, and analyzing information about user behavior. Understanding how secure browsing works and how online tracking operates is essential for anyone seeking greater privacy and security on mobile devices.

Mobile browsing has become one of the most common digital activities worldwide. Smartphones allow users to access information instantly from virtually anywhere. Whether using a dedicated browser application or viewing web content through mobile apps, internet activity generates data that can be collected and analyzed. While some data collection is necessary for website functionality, other forms of tracking are designed primarily for advertising, profiling, analytics, or behavioral monitoring purposes.

The first step toward secure browsing is understanding what information websites can potentially collect. When a user visits a website, the site may gather information such as the visitor's IP address, device type, operating system, browser version, screen size, language settings, location information, browsing behavior, and referral sources. Individually, some of these data points may appear harmless. However, when combined, they can create detailed profiles of individual users and their online habits.

One of the most common tracking technologies is the browser cookie. Cookies are small text files stored on a device by websites. Some cookies serve legitimate purposes, such as remembering login sessions, shopping cart contents, language preferences, or website settings. These are often referred to as first-party cookies because they originate from the website the user is visiting.

Third-party cookies operate differently. These cookies are typically placed by advertising networks, analytics services, or external content providers embedded within websites. Third-party cookies can track users across multiple websites, allowing advertisers and data brokers to build detailed profiles based on browsing activity over time. This information is often used to deliver targeted advertisements and personalized content.

While cookies have received significant attention, they represent only one method of online tracking. Modern tracking systems employ a wide range of techniques that may not rely on cookies at all. Browser fingerprinting is one such technique. Browser fingerprinting collects information about a device's configuration, including browser settings, installed fonts, screen resolution, time zone, language preferences, and other characteristics. When combined, these attributes can create a unique digital fingerprint capable of identifying users even when cookies are blocked or deleted.

Mobile applications frequently contribute to tracking activities as well. Many apps include software development kits, often called SDKs, that collect analytics and advertising information. These embedded components may transmit data about app usage, device identifiers, location information, user behavior, and interactions with advertisements. As a result, privacy protection requires attention not only to web browsers but also to mobile applications themselves.

Secure browsing begins with selecting a trustworthy browser. Modern browsers offer varying levels of privacy protection, security features, and customization options. Some browsers prioritize convenience and ecosystem integration, while others focus heavily on privacy and minimizing data collection. Users should evaluate browsers based on security update frequency, privacy controls, tracking protection features, and overall reputation.

Regular software updates are among the most important security measures for any browser. Cybercriminals continuously search for vulnerabilities that can be exploited to compromise devices or steal information. Browser developers routinely release updates that patch discovered weaknesses and improve security protections. Failing to install updates may leave users vulnerable to known threats that have already been addressed by developers.

HTTPS technology plays a critical role in secure browsing. Secure websites use HTTPS to encrypt communications between the browser and web server. This encryption helps protect sensitive information such as passwords, financial data, personal messages, and account credentials while they are transmitted across networks. Users should verify that websites requesting personal information utilize secure HTTPS connections before submitting sensitive data.

Although HTTPS improves security, users should understand its limitations. HTTPS protects data during transmission but does not guarantee that a website itself is trustworthy. A fraudulent website can still obtain an HTTPS certificate and display a secure connection indicator. Therefore, users should remain cautious when visiting unfamiliar websites, clicking links in emails, or responding to unsolicited messages requesting personal information.

Private browsing modes are another commonly misunderstood feature. Most modern browsers offer private or incognito modes that limit local storage of browsing history, cookies, and session data. While these modes provide some privacy benefits on the device itself, they do not make users anonymous online. Internet service providers, websites, employers, schools, and network administrators may still be able to observe browsing activity depending on the circumstances.

Search engines also play a significant role in online privacy. Traditional search engines often collect extensive information about user queries, search history, interests, and browsing behavior. Privacy-focused search engines seek to minimize data collection and reduce user profiling. While no service can eliminate all forms of tracking, privacy-oriented search providers can help reduce the amount of personal information shared during routine internet searches.

Advertisement tracking represents one of the largest sources of online data collection. Advertising networks monitor browsing behavior across websites and applications to create detailed user profiles. These profiles may include interests, demographics, shopping preferences, browsing patterns, and behavioral predictions. Mobile users who value privacy should familiarize themselves with advertising controls, tracking permissions, and privacy settings available on their devices.

Many browsers now include built-in tracker-blocking features that help prevent third-party trackers from collecting information. Some privacy-focused browsers automatically block known tracking domains, advertising scripts, fingerprinting attempts, and malicious content. These protections can improve both privacy and browsing performance by reducing unnecessary background activity.

Secure DNS services provide another layer of protection. DNS, or Domain Name System, translates website names into numerical addresses used by computers. Traditional DNS requests may be visible to internet service providers or network operators. Secure DNS technologies encrypt these requests, reducing exposure and helping protect browsing privacy.

Users should also be aware of phishing websites designed to steal credentials and sensitive information. Phishing sites often imitate legitimate organizations such as banks, social media platforms, government agencies, or online retailers. Attackers use deceptive emails, messages, advertisements, or search results to lure victims into entering usernames, passwords, financial information, or personal details.

Recognizing phishing attempts requires careful attention. Users should verify website addresses, examine domain names, avoid clicking suspicious links, and navigate directly to important websites whenever possible. Even sophisticated phishing attacks often contain subtle inconsistencies that attentive users can identify.

Public Wi-Fi networks introduce additional browsing risks. Cybercriminals may attempt to intercept traffic, redirect users to malicious websites, or exploit insecure network configurations. Combining secure browsing practices with VPN protection helps reduce exposure when using public networks. VPNs encrypt internet traffic and add an additional layer of privacy between the device and external networks.

Mobile browsers often offer security settings that users overlook. Features such as fraud protection, secure DNS, tracker blocking, pop-up controls, download scanning, and permission management can significantly improve browsing security when properly configured. Spending time reviewing browser settings can yield meaningful privacy and security benefits.

Ultimately, secure browsing involves more than simply installing a browser or activating a privacy setting. It requires understanding how online tracking operates, recognizing potential threats, making informed choices about digital services, and maintaining consistent security habits. By combining secure browsers, privacy-focused tools, encrypted connections, careful browsing behavior, and ongoing awareness, users can significantly improve both their privacy and security while navigating the modern internet.

As mobile technology continues to evolve, so will tracking systems and online threats. However, users who understand the principles discussed in this chapter will be better prepared to protect themselves from excessive data collection, online surveillance, malicious websites, and privacy violations. Secure browsing is not about becoming invisible online but about maintaining greater control over personal information and reducing unnecessary exposure in an increasingly connected world.

Sophia found the advertisements amusing

Sophia enjoyed spending time online. Her smartphone served as her primary gateway to news, shopping, social media, entertainment, education, and communication. Whether waiting in line, commuting, relaxing at home, or traveling, she frequently used her mobile browser to explore information and stay connected.

Like many people, Sophia rarely thought about what happened behind the scenes when she visited websites. She assumed that browsing was a private activity involving only herself and the sites she intentionally visited. The idea that dozens of companies might be monitoring her online behavior never crossed her mind.

One evening, while searching for hiking equipment, Sophia noticed something unusual. After viewing a few backpacks online, advertisements for hiking gear began appearing everywhere. Social media feeds displayed camping equipment. News websites featured outdoor clothing promotions. Video platforms recommended hiking-related products.

At first, Sophia found the advertisements amusing. However, as the pattern continued over several weeks, she became increasingly curious. How did so many companies know what she had been browsing?

Determined to find answers, she enrolled in a community technology workshop focused on digital privacy. The instructor, a cybersecurity specialist named Carlos, explained how online tracking systems operated. He described cookies, advertising networks, browser fingerprinting, analytics platforms, and data collection practices used throughout the modern internet.

Sophia was astonished by what she learned.

Carlos demonstrated how websites often communicate with numerous third-party services behind the scenes. A single webpage might load advertising scripts, analytics tools, social media integrations, video players, tracking pixels, and external content providers. Each component could potentially collect information about user behavior.

After the workshop, Sophia began investigating her own digital habits. She reviewed browser settings, application permissions, privacy options, and advertising preferences. The process revealed a surprising amount of data sharing occurring across multiple services.

Rather than becoming fearful, Sophia approached the situation as a learning opportunity. She installed a privacy-focused browser that included tracker-blocking features. She adjusted cookie settings, enabled secure DNS, reviewed app permissions, and began using privacy-conscious search tools. She also learned how to identify secure HTTPS connections and recognize suspicious websites.

The changes produced noticeable results. Webpages loaded more quickly because many tracking scripts were blocked. Advertisements became less personalized. She felt more confident knowing that unnecessary data collection had been reduced.

Several months later, Sophia received an email claiming to be from her bank. The message warned of suspicious account activity and urged her to click a link immediately to verify her credentials.

Before attending Carlos's workshop, she likely would have clicked the link without hesitation. This time, however, she paused.

Carefully examining the email, she noticed subtle inconsistencies. The sender address appeared unusual. The wording felt slightly different from previous bank communications. Most importantly, the website address associated with the link did not exactly match her bank's official domain.

Instead of clicking, Sophia opened her banking application directly and logged in through official channels. Everything appeared normal. She then contacted customer support, which confirmed that the email was a phishing attempt targeting customers.

The experience reinforced the importance of awareness. Technology alone had not protected her. Education and critical thinking had played equally important roles.

Later that year, Sophia helped her parents improve their online security. She explained concepts such as secure browsing, tracker blocking, phishing awareness, and privacy settings. Initially, they worried that cybersecurity would be too technical or difficult to understand.

Sophia reassured them by focusing on practical habits rather than technical details. She showed them how to recognize secure websites, avoid suspicious links, update browsers regularly, and review privacy settings. Gradually, they became more comfortable navigating the internet safely.

One afternoon, her father called excitedly after identifying a phishing message that he previously would have trusted. He proudly explained how he noticed inconsistencies in the sender address and avoided clicking the fraudulent link.

Sophia smiled because she realized how much confidence simple knowledge could provide. Cybersecurity was no longer a mysterious subject reserved for experts. It had become a set of practical skills that ordinary people could learn and apply.

Years later, Sophia reflected on her journey. The internet remained an incredible resource for learning, communication, and opportunity. She continued to enjoy browsing, shopping, researching, and connecting with others online. The difference was that she now understood how the digital ecosystem operated.

She recognized that websites, advertisers, and technology companies often collected information. She understood how tracking systems worked and how privacy tools reduced exposure. Most importantly, she knew how to make informed choices about the services she used.

Rather than feeling powerless, Sophia felt empowered. Secure browsing had given her greater control over her personal information and online experiences. While complete privacy might never be achievable, thoughtful habits and effective tools allowed her to significantly reduce unnecessary data collection and protect herself from many common threats.

Her experience illustrated an important lesson. Online privacy is not achieved through a single application or setting. It develops through awareness, education, and consistent action. By understanding how tracking works and adopting secure browsing practices, individuals can navigate the digital world with greater confidence, security, and peace of mind.

Chapter 5

Privacy Apps, Secure Messaging, and Building a Complete Mobile Privacy System

Protecting privacy on a mobile device requires more than using a VPN or choosing a secure browser. While those tools provide important layers of protection, modern mobile security depends upon a comprehensive approach that addresses communication, data storage, authentication, application permissions, device security, and online behavior. Cybercriminals, advertisers, data brokers, and surveillance systems often collect information from multiple sources simultaneously. Therefore, users who wish to improve their privacy must think in terms of building an entire privacy ecosystem rather than relying on a single solution.

A complete mobile privacy system consists of several interconnected layers working together. These layers include device security, encrypted communications, secure browsing, VPN protection, privacy-focused applications, strong authentication, encrypted backups, and safe user habits. Each layer contributes to overall security, and weaknesses in one area can potentially undermine protections in another. The goal is not perfection but rather reducing unnecessary exposure and creating multiple barriers against threats.

One of the most important components of a privacy-focused mobile environment is secure messaging. Communication applications have become central to daily life. People use messaging apps to exchange personal conversations, business information, financial details, photographs, videos, and sensitive documents. Because of the amount of information shared through these platforms, choosing secure communication tools is essential.

When evaluating messaging applications, users should understand the difference between standard encryption and end-to-end encryption. Standard encryption often protects messages while they travel between devices and servers. However, service providers may still be capable of accessing message contents on their systems. End-to-end encryption offers stronger protection by ensuring that only the sender and recipient can read the messages. Even the service provider cannot access properly encrypted content.

End-to-end encryption significantly improves privacy because it reduces the number of parties capable of accessing communications. If a service provider experiences a breach, attackers may be unable to read encrypted conversations.

Likewise, unauthorized insiders or external observers face greater difficulty accessing protected communications. For users discussing personal, financial, medical, legal, or business matters, end-to-end encryption provides valuable safeguards.

Users should also pay attention to metadata when selecting communication tools. Even when message content is encrypted, metadata may reveal information about communication patterns. Metadata can include contact relationships, communication frequency, timestamps, device information, and network details. Some privacy-focused messaging services attempt to minimize metadata collection in addition to protecting message content.

Secure email services represent another important privacy consideration. Traditional email systems often prioritize convenience and compatibility over privacy. Messages may be stored on servers for extended periods and could potentially be accessible under certain circumstances. Privacy-oriented email providers typically emphasize encryption, reduced tracking, stronger security controls, and improved user privacy. While email remains an important communication tool, users should recognize its limitations and choose services appropriate for their needs.

Password managers are another critical component of a complete privacy system. Many security incidents result from weak, reused, or stolen passwords. Unfortunately, remembering strong and unique passwords for dozens or even hundreds of accounts is nearly impossible without assistance. Password managers solve this problem by securely storing credentials within encrypted vaults protected by a master password.

A high-quality password manager allows users to generate strong passwords, store login credentials securely, and synchronize information across trusted devices. By using unique passwords for every account, users reduce the risk that a compromise affecting one service will expose additional accounts. Password managers improve both security and convenience, making them one of the most valuable privacy tools available.

Multi-factor authentication strengthens account protection even further. Authentication factors generally fall into three categories: something you know, something you have, and something you are. Passwords represent something you know. Authentication applications, security keys, or mobile devices represent something you have. Biometric factors such as fingerprints or facial recognition represent something you are.

By requiring multiple factors, multi-factor authentication significantly reduces the likelihood of unauthorized account access. Even if attackers obtain a password through phishing, data breaches, or malware, they may still be unable to access the account without the additional verification factor. Whenever available, users should enable multi-factor authentication for important accounts.

Cloud storage services deserve careful evaluation as part of any privacy strategy. Cloud platforms provide convenient access to files, backups, photographs, and documents from multiple devices. However, privacy protections vary among providers. Some services retain access to encryption keys, while others offer zero-knowledge architectures in which only the user controls access to encrypted data.

Users storing sensitive information should understand how their cloud provider handles encryption, authentication, data retention, and account recovery processes. Strong privacy protections often involve balancing convenience with security. In some situations, additional encryption measures may be appropriate before uploading highly sensitive information.

Mobile device permissions represent another important area of privacy management. Applications often request access to device features such as cameras, microphones, contacts, location services, calendars, storage, and notifications. While some permissions are necessary for functionality, others may collect information unrelated to the app's primary purpose.

Regularly reviewing app permissions allows users to identify unnecessary access and reduce data exposure. For example, a weather application may require approximate location access, but it generally does not need access to contact lists or microphone functionality. Limiting permissions reduces opportunities for excessive data collection and strengthens privacy controls.

Location privacy has become increasingly important in modern mobile environments. Smartphones continuously generate location-related information through GPS, Wi-Fi networks, cellular towers, Bluetooth systems, and application activity. Many apps request location access even when such information is not essential for functionality. Users should carefully evaluate location permissions and consider whether continuous tracking is truly necessary.

Encrypted backups provide protection against data loss while maintaining privacy. Mobile devices may be lost, stolen, damaged, or infected with malware. Secure backups ensure that important information remains recoverable. However, backups should be protected using strong encryption and authentication measures to prevent unauthorized access. Users should verify that backup systems meet appropriate security standards.

Privacy-focused browsers, VPNs, secure DNS services, encrypted messaging platforms, password managers, and authentication tools work best when combined into a unified system. Each layer addresses specific risks while complementing other protections. For example, a VPN protects internet traffic, but it does not secure weak passwords. A password manager protects credentials, but it does not encrypt communications. A secure messaging application protects conversations, but it does not prevent device theft. Together, these tools create a more comprehensive security posture.

User behavior remains one of the most important factors in mobile privacy. Even the best tools cannot fully protect individuals who ignore security warnings, click suspicious links, share sensitive information carelessly, or install untrusted software. Privacy-conscious users develop habits that support security objectives. These habits include verifying website authenticity, reviewing permissions, updating software promptly, enabling security features, and remaining cautious when interacting with unknown contacts.

Another important principle involves minimizing unnecessary data collection. Every piece of information shared online creates potential exposure. Users should consider whether requested information is truly necessary before providing it. Reducing data sharing not only improves privacy but also limits the impact of potential breaches or misuse.

Privacy is often misunderstood as secrecy. In reality, privacy involves maintaining control over personal information and deciding how that information is used. Most individuals are not attempting to hide wrongdoing. Rather, they seek reasonable protection for personal communications, financial data, professional activities, family information, and digital identities. Privacy tools help support this objective by limiting unnecessary exposure and strengthening user control.

As technology continues evolving, privacy challenges will likely become more complex. Artificial intelligence systems, advanced analytics platforms, behavioral profiling technologies, and expanding data ecosystems will continue generating new concerns. However, the core principles of privacy remain remarkably consistent. Strong encryption, secure communications, responsible data management, and informed decision-making will continue serving as the foundation of effective mobile security.

Building a complete mobile privacy system is not a one-time project but an ongoing process. Users should periodically review settings, evaluate applications, update security practices, and adapt to emerging threats. By combining appropriate tools with consistent habits, individuals can significantly improve their privacy while maintaining the convenience and functionality that make smartphones such valuable devices.

The ultimate goal is confidence. Users who understand privacy principles and implement layered protections can navigate the digital world with greater assurance. Rather than fearing technology, they can use it productively while maintaining control over their personal information, communications, and digital lives.

Daniel had reused the same password across numerous services

Daniel owned a small consulting business that relied heavily on mobile technology. His smartphone served as his office, communication center, banking terminal, project management tool, and personal organizer. Nearly every aspect of his life flowed through a single device.

For years, Daniel believed that installing antivirus software was sufficient to keep him safe. Beyond that, he rarely considered privacy or security. He used the same password for multiple accounts, granted application permissions without reading them, and assumed that technology companies handled security on his behalf.

One morning, Daniel received an alert indicating that one of his online accounts had experienced suspicious login attempts. Shortly afterward, he learned that another service he used had suffered a data breach exposing customer information. Although none of his accounts were immediately compromised, the incidents made him uncomfortable.

Seeking guidance, Daniel attended a local cybersecurity seminar. The instructor, a mobile security specialist named Rachel, discussed privacy protection, secure communications, password management, and digital resilience. Rather than focusing on fear, Rachel emphasized practical strategies that ordinary people could implement.

One statement particularly resonated with Daniel.

"Privacy is not a single tool," Rachel explained. "It's a system."

After the seminar, Daniel approached her and described his concerns. Rachel suggested conducting a complete review of his mobile security environment. Together, they examined his device settings, communication tools, passwords, application permissions, cloud storage practices, and authentication methods.

The results were eye-opening.

Daniel had reused the same password across numerous services. Several applications possessed extensive permissions unrelated to their functionality. Sensitive business documents were stored in locations with minimal protection. Multi-factor authentication was disabled on important accounts. Communication tools varied significantly in their privacy features.

Rather than becoming overwhelmed, Daniel decided to make gradual improvements.

His first step involved installing a password manager. Initially, he worried that managing passwords would become complicated. Instead, the password manager simplified his life by generating and storing strong credentials automatically. Within a few weeks, every major account used a unique password.

Next, he enabled multi-factor authentication wherever possible. Although the extra verification step added a few seconds to account access, he appreciated the additional protection. Knowing that a stolen password alone could not compromise his accounts provided significant peace of mind.

Daniel then reviewed application permissions. He discovered several apps collecting location information unnecessarily. Others requested access to contacts, microphones, or storage despite having little legitimate need for such permissions. He adjusted settings accordingly and removed several applications altogether.

As his confidence grew, he explored secure messaging platforms and privacy-focused communication tools. Rachel helped him understand the differences between standard encryption and end-to-end encryption. He began using secure communication methods for sensitive business discussions and client interactions.

Several months later, one of Daniel's colleagues experienced a serious phishing attack. The attacker obtained login credentials and attempted to access multiple business systems. Fortunately, multi-factor authentication prevented unauthorized access. The incident reinforced the value of layered security measures.

Daniel realized that no single tool had protected his colleague. Instead, multiple defenses worked together. Passwords, authentication controls, user awareness, and security monitoring collectively prevented a potentially damaging breach.

Inspired by his progress, Daniel expanded his privacy efforts. He configured encrypted backups, adopted a VPN for public Wi-Fi use, reviewed cloud storage settings, and implemented stronger device security controls. Each improvement contributed another layer to his overall privacy system.

One afternoon, while meeting with a prospective client, the conversation turned to cybersecurity concerns. The client worried about protecting sensitive business information in an increasingly connected world.

Daniel shared his experiences and explained how he had transformed his approach to mobile security. Rather than recommending a specific product, he emphasized the importance of creating a complete privacy ecosystem. Secure communication, strong authentication, responsible permissions management, and encrypted storage all played important roles.

The client appreciated the practical advice because it focused on achievable improvements rather than technical complexity. Daniel realized that many people shared similar concerns but often lacked clear guidance on where to begin.

Over time, privacy became a routine part of Daniel's daily habits rather than an occasional concern. He reviewed permissions periodically, monitored account security, updated applications promptly, and remained cautious when sharing information online. These actions required minimal effort yet provided substantial benefits.

Years later, Daniel reflected on how much his perspective had changed. Initially, he viewed privacy as a specialized topic relevant only to cybersecurity professionals. Now he understood that privacy affected everyone who used a smartphone, communicated online, stored digital information, or interacted with modern technology.

Most importantly, he recognized that privacy was not about hiding. It was about maintaining control. It was about deciding who could access personal information, when that access occurred, and how data was used. Privacy tools helped support those choices by creating barriers against unnecessary exposure.

As technology continued evolving, Daniel remained committed to adapting his practices. New threats would emerge, new tools would become available, and new challenges would arise. Yet the principles Rachel had taught him remained constant.

Build layers of protection. Minimize unnecessary exposure. Verify before trusting. Protect important information. Stay informed.

Those principles formed the foundation of his mobile privacy system and allowed him to navigate the digital world with confidence. Rather than worrying about every potential threat, he focused on maintaining strong habits and using appropriate tools. In doing so, he achieved the true goal of privacy—not secrecy, but control, security, and peace of mind in an increasingly connected world.

Chapter 6

Advanced Mobile Privacy Strategies and Creating Your Long-Term Digital Protection Plan

By this point in the book, you have learned how VPNs protect internet traffic, how encryption secures communications and data, how secure browsing reduces online exposure, and how privacy-focused applications contribute to a safer mobile environment. The final step is bringing all these elements together into a long-term privacy strategy. Mobile privacy is not a one-time setup or a single security feature. It is an ongoing process that evolves alongside technology, user behavior, and emerging threats. The most secure users are not necessarily those with the most advanced tools but those who consistently apply sound security principles over time.

One of the most important concepts in advanced privacy protection is understanding your personal threat model. A threat model refers to the specific risks, adversaries, and vulnerabilities relevant to an individual. Not everyone faces the same privacy challenges. A student, business owner, journalist, healthcare professional, traveler, parent, and government employee may all require different levels of protection. Understanding your personal situation allows you to make informed decisions about which privacy measures are appropriate for your needs.

For most mobile users, the primary threats include identity theft, phishing attacks, account compromise, financial fraud, excessive tracking, data collection, malware infections, and unauthorized access to personal information. Recognizing these common risks helps users prioritize the protections that will have the greatest impact. Rather than attempting to eliminate every possible risk, users should focus on reducing the threats most likely to affect their daily lives.

Digital minimalism is another valuable privacy strategy. Digital minimalism involves reducing unnecessary exposure by limiting the amount of information collected, stored, and shared. Many users accumulate dozens of applications, accounts, subscriptions, and online profiles over time. Each additional service potentially increases the attack surface available to cybercriminals and data collectors. Periodically reviewing and removing unused accounts, applications, and services helps improve privacy while simplifying digital life.

Account management plays a critical role in long-term security. Many individuals create online accounts and then forget about them. These abandoned accounts may continue storing personal information and could become targets for attackers if security measures are weak. Users should regularly review active accounts, update passwords, enable multi-factor authentication, and close accounts that are no longer needed.

Device lifecycle management is another important aspect of privacy planning. Smartphones have finite lifespans. As devices age, manufacturers may eventually stop providing security updates. Once updates cease, newly discovered vulnerabilities may remain unpatched, increasing security risks. Users should consider the security support period when purchasing devices and plan for replacement before support ends.

Mobile operating system updates remain one of the most effective security measures available. Developers continuously identify and fix vulnerabilities that could otherwise be exploited by attackers. Delaying updates unnecessarily may leave devices exposed to threats that have already been addressed through official patches. Users should establish a habit of installing updates promptly while ensuring that important data is backed up beforehand.

Privacy-conscious users should also understand data retention practices. Many online services store information indefinitely unless users actively delete it. Emails, messages, photographs, search histories, location records, and account activity may remain accessible for years. Reviewing data retention settings and deleting unnecessary information helps reduce exposure while improving control over personal data.

Location privacy deserves special attention in long-term security planning. Smartphones generate vast amounts of location-related information through GPS systems, wireless networks, Bluetooth devices, and application activity. Over time, location histories can reveal detailed patterns about daily routines, workplaces, homes, travel habits, and personal relationships. Users should periodically review location permissions and disable unnecessary tracking whenever possible.

Social engineering remains one of the most effective techniques used by cybercriminals. Unlike technical attacks, social engineering targets human behavior. Attackers may impersonate trusted organizations, create fake emergencies, exploit curiosity, or manipulate emotions to obtain sensitive information. Advanced privacy protection requires developing skepticism toward unsolicited communications and verifying requests independently before taking action.

Artificial intelligence is increasingly influencing both cybersecurity and privacy. AI-powered systems can analyze large volumes of data, identify behavioral patterns, and automate decision-making processes. While AI offers many benefits, it also introduces new privacy considerations. Users should understand how organizations collect and process data used by AI systems and review privacy policies associated with AI-enabled applications and services.

Data brokers represent another significant privacy concern. These organizations collect information from numerous sources, including public records, commercial transactions, websites, mobile applications, loyalty programs, and advertising networks. Data brokers often compile detailed profiles that may include demographic information, purchasing behavior, interests, location history, and online activities. While eliminating all data broker collection may be difficult, privacy-conscious users can reduce exposure by limiting unnecessary data sharing and utilizing available opt-out mechanisms where appropriate.

Secure backups remain a cornerstone of digital resilience. Privacy protection is not solely about preventing unauthorized access; it is also about ensuring continued access to important information when devices fail, are lost, or become compromised. Effective backup strategies include redundancy, encryption, secure storage locations, and regular testing. Users should verify that backup systems function properly before emergencies occur.

Families and households should consider privacy as a shared responsibility. One individual's weak security practices can affect others connected through shared accounts, family devices, communication channels, or financial systems. Establishing household security guidelines helps create a stronger collective defense. Topics may include password management, phishing awareness, application permissions, software updates, and safe browsing practices.

Children and teenagers require special attention within family privacy planning. Younger users may not fully understand online risks and often adopt new applications or services without considering privacy implications. Parents should balance supervision with education, teaching children how to make responsible digital decisions while gradually developing cybersecurity awareness.

Travel introduces unique privacy challenges. International travel often involves unfamiliar networks, public charging stations, foreign regulations, and increased opportunities for surveillance or theft. Privacy-conscious travelers should use VPNs, avoid untrusted charging stations, secure devices physically, enable remote management features, and limit unnecessary exposure of sensitive information while away from home.

Another advanced strategy involves conducting periodic privacy audits. A privacy audit is a structured review of devices, accounts, applications, permissions, passwords, backups, and security settings. Performing audits every few months helps identify weaknesses before they become serious problems. Users should verify that privacy tools remain functional, update outdated settings, and address newly discovered risks.

The principle of defense in depth remains central to effective mobile privacy. Defense in depth refers to implementing multiple layers of protection rather than relying on a single safeguard. If one layer fails, additional controls continue providing protection. For example, a phishing attack may compromise a password, but multi-factor authentication may prevent account access. A stolen device may expose hardware, but encryption protects stored data. Public Wi-Fi may be insecure, but a VPN protects network traffic.

Privacy should ultimately be viewed as an ongoing process of risk management rather than a destination. No system can guarantee complete anonymity or perfect security. New technologies, evolving threats, and changing user behaviors constantly reshape the digital landscape. However, users who understand privacy principles and apply them consistently can significantly reduce risk while maintaining control over their personal information.

The goal of long-term privacy planning is confidence and resilience. Confidence comes from understanding how technologies work and knowing that appropriate protections are in place. Resilience comes from preparing for unexpected events and ensuring that problems can be managed effectively when they occur. Together, these qualities enable users to benefit from technology while maintaining a strong privacy posture.

As you conclude this book, remember that privacy is not achieved through fear or extreme measures. It is achieved through awareness, thoughtful decision-making, responsible habits, and appropriate tools. By applying the concepts discussed throughout this book, you can build a sustainable mobile privacy strategy that protects your information, supports your goals, and adapts to future challenges.

Nathan decided to conduct a complete review of his digital life

Nathan had always considered himself reasonably careful with technology. He used antivirus software, updated his smartphone occasionally, and avoided obviously suspicious websites. For many years, he believed these basic precautions were enough.

As a project manager for a growing engineering company, Nathan relied heavily on his smartphone. It contained business communications, client information, financial applications, family photographs, travel itineraries, and access to numerous online accounts. His device had become an extension of both his professional and personal life.

One day, while attending a cybersecurity awareness seminar organized by his employer, Nathan heard a phrase that captured his attention.

"Privacy is not a product. Privacy is a process."

The presenter, a security consultant named Laura, explained that many people purchase security tools expecting immediate protection. While those tools can be valuable, long-term security depends on consistent habits and informed decisions.

Nathan found himself reflecting on his own practices. Although he had installed some security software years earlier, he rarely reviewed settings, updated passwords, or examined account activity. He assumed everything was functioning properly simply because no major problems had occurred.

Inspired by the seminar, Nathan decided to conduct a complete review of his digital life.

He began by examining the applications installed on his smartphone. To his surprise, dozens of unused apps remained on the device. Some had not been opened in years. Many retained permissions for location access, contacts, storage, and other sensitive information.

Over the next several evenings, Nathan carefully reviewed each application. Unused apps were removed. Permissions were adjusted. Privacy settings were updated. The process felt surprisingly satisfying because it reduced clutter while improving security.

Next, Nathan turned his attention to online accounts. He discovered accounts associated with old services, forgotten subscriptions, and websites he no longer used. Some accounts contained outdated personal information and weak passwords created years earlier.

Using a password manager, he generated unique credentials and enabled multi-factor authentication wherever possible. Accounts that no longer served a purpose were closed entirely. Gradually, his digital footprint became smaller and easier to manage.

Several months later, Nathan experienced an unexpected challenge. During a family vacation, his smartphone disappeared while visiting a crowded tourist attraction. Panic set in immediately. The device contained years of personal and professional information.

Fortunately, Nathan had prepared for this possibility.

Device encryption was enabled. Remote management features were active. Secure backups existed. Multi-factor authentication protected important accounts. Within hours, he remotely locked the device and initiated recovery procedures.

Although the phone was never recovered, the incident caused far less disruption than it otherwise might have. Most importantly, sensitive information remained protected.

The experience reinforced the importance of resilience. Nathan realized that effective privacy planning was not merely about preventing incidents. It was also about ensuring that problems could be managed when they occurred.

Upon returning home, he shared the experience with his family. Together, they reviewed household security practices. His wife updated account protections. His teenage daughter learned about privacy settings and phishing scams. The family established simple guidelines for password management, software updates, and online safety.

Over time, cybersecurity became a regular topic of discussion rather than an occasional concern. Family members shared suspicious messages, verified unusual requests, and helped one another identify potential risks. Security evolved into a shared responsibility.

Years later, Nathan attended another seminar led by Laura. After the presentation, he approached her and described how her advice had transformed his approach to privacy.

Laura listened carefully and smiled.

"The most successful security strategy is the one people actually maintain," she said.

Nathan understood exactly what she meant.

Many people searched for perfect solutions or magical technologies that would eliminate all risk. In reality, security involved consistent effort, informed decisions, and practical habits. Small actions performed regularly often provided greater protection than complex tools used inconsistently.

As technology continued advancing, Nathan remained committed to adapting his practices. He reviewed new privacy features, evaluated emerging threats, and adjusted his strategies when necessary. Yet the core principles remained unchanged.

Protect what matters most.

Limit unnecessary exposure.

Prepare for unexpected events.

Verify before trusting.

Use multiple layers of protection.

Stay informed.

These principles became the foundation of his long-term digital protection plan.

Looking back, Nathan realized that privacy was not about hiding from the world. It was about preserving freedom, maintaining control, and protecting the information that shaped his life. Technology would continue evolving, bringing both opportunities and risks. But with knowledge, preparation, and discipline, he felt confident navigating whatever challenges the future might bring.

His journey demonstrated a lesson that applies to every smartphone user. Privacy is not a destination reached once and forgotten. It is an ongoing commitment to protecting personal information, adapting to change, and making thoughtful decisions in an increasingly connected world.

Through awareness, planning, and consistent action, anyone can build a strong foundation for digital security. And that foundation provides something increasingly valuable in the modern age: confidence, control, and peace of mind.

Chapter 7

Mobile Privacy Action Plan and Building a Lifetime of Secure Digital Habits

The technologies discussed throughout this book—including VPNs, encryption, secure browsers, privacy-focused applications, password managers, multi-factor authentication systems, and secure backups—provide powerful tools for protecting personal information. However, technology alone cannot guarantee privacy. The most effective long-term defense comes from developing secure habits that become part of daily life. Just as physical health depends on consistent lifestyle choices rather than occasional actions, digital privacy depends on routine behaviors that reduce risk and strengthen security over time.

Many people approach cybersecurity reactively. They become interested in security only after experiencing a phishing attack, account compromise, identity theft incident, malware infection, or financial fraud. While learning from experience can be valuable, proactive preparation is far more effective. A well-designed privacy action plan allows users to identify vulnerabilities, implement protections, and reduce exposure before problems occur. Prevention is almost always easier, less expensive, and less stressful than recovery.

The first step in creating a mobile privacy action plan is taking inventory of your digital environment. Most smartphone users interact with dozens or even hundreds of services. These may include email accounts, social media platforms, banking applications, cloud storage providers, messaging services, streaming subscriptions, shopping websites, professional tools, educational platforms, and government services. Understanding what information is stored where is essential for effective privacy management.

Many users are surprised by how many accounts they maintain. Over time, accounts accumulate through daily activities, promotions, free trials, purchases, and changing interests. Some accounts remain active for years despite no longer serving a useful purpose. Each account potentially stores personal information and represents a possible target for cybercriminals. Conducting a comprehensive account inventory helps users identify unnecessary exposure and prioritize security improvements.

Once accounts have been identified, users should classify them according to importance and sensitivity. Financial accounts, primary email accounts, healthcare portals, business systems, tax services, and cloud storage platforms generally require the highest level of protection. Social media accounts, entertainment subscriptions, and less sensitive services may still require security measures but often represent lower risk. Understanding these distinctions helps allocate security resources efficiently.

Email security deserves particular attention because email accounts often function as the foundation of digital identity. Password reset links, account notifications, authentication codes, financial communications, and personal correspondence frequently pass through email systems. If an attacker gains access to a primary email account, numerous connected services may become vulnerable. Therefore, strong passwords, multi-factor authentication, and careful monitoring are especially important for email security.

The next stage of a privacy action plan involves strengthening authentication practices. Every important account should use a unique password generated through a reputable password manager. Reusing passwords across multiple services creates significant risk because a compromise affecting one platform can expose credentials usable elsewhere. Password managers eliminate the need to memorize dozens of complex passwords while improving overall security.

Multi-factor authentication should be enabled wherever available, particularly for high-value accounts. Authentication applications are generally preferable to text-message-based authentication because they provide stronger protection against certain attacks. Security keys offer even greater protection for users requiring advanced security. Regardless of the method chosen, adding an additional verification factor significantly improves account security.

Device security forms another essential component of the action plan. Smartphones should be protected by strong passcodes, biometric authentication, device encryption, and automatic locking mechanisms. These protections reduce the risk associated with device loss or theft. Users should also enable device location services and remote management features that allow devices to be located, locked, or erased if necessary.

Application management is equally important. Users should periodically review installed applications and remove those that are no longer needed. Every installed application introduces potential privacy and security considerations. Fewer applications generally mean fewer opportunities for data collection, vulnerabilities, and unnecessary permissions. Regular app reviews help maintain a cleaner and more secure mobile environment.

Permission management should accompany application reviews. Users should examine which applications have access to location services, microphones, cameras, contacts, calendars, storage systems, and other sensitive resources. Permissions should be granted only when necessary for legitimate functionality. Limiting access reduces the amount of information available to third parties and minimizes potential privacy risks.

Secure browsing habits are another critical aspect of long-term privacy protection. Users should verify website authenticity before entering sensitive information, pay attention to HTTPS connections, avoid suspicious links, and remain cautious when responding to unsolicited communications. Browser privacy settings should be reviewed periodically, and tracking protections should be enabled whenever practical.

VPN usage should become routine whenever connecting to unfamiliar or public networks. Airports, hotels, conference centers, libraries, restaurants, and coffee shops often provide convenient internet access, but they may also expose users to additional risks. VPNs help protect internet traffic by encrypting communications and reducing exposure to network monitoring. Automatic VPN activation features can simplify this process and ensure consistent protection.

Data backup strategies must also be incorporated into the action plan. Backups protect against device failures, theft, accidental deletion, ransomware attacks, and other forms of data loss. Effective backup systems include redundancy, encryption, secure storage locations, and periodic testing. Users should verify that backups function properly and contain important information before emergencies occur.

Privacy-conscious users should establish a schedule for regular security reviews. Monthly reviews might focus on software updates and account activity. Quarterly reviews could include permission audits, password evaluations, backup verification, and privacy setting assessments. Annual reviews may involve more comprehensive evaluations of accounts, applications, devices, and security strategies. Regular reviews help identify issues before they become serious problems.

Education remains one of the most powerful cybersecurity tools available. Threats evolve continuously as attackers develop new techniques and technologies. Staying informed about emerging scams, phishing methods, malware trends, and privacy concerns allows users to adapt their defenses accordingly. Continuous learning strengthens decision-making and improves resilience against future threats.

Families should incorporate privacy education into household routines. Children and teenagers increasingly rely on smartphones for communication, entertainment, education, and social interaction. Teaching younger users about privacy, phishing awareness, password management, application permissions, and responsible online behavior helps establish positive habits early in life. Family discussions about digital safety should be ongoing rather than limited to occasional warnings.

The concept of digital resilience is especially important. Resilience refers to the ability to recover from setbacks and continue functioning effectively after disruptions occur. No security system is perfect. Devices may be lost, accounts may be targeted, and mistakes may happen. A resilient privacy strategy includes contingency plans, backups, recovery procedures, and realistic expectations. The goal is not perfection but preparedness.

Another valuable habit involves minimizing unnecessary data sharing. Before providing information to websites, applications, surveys, promotions, or online services, users should ask whether the requested information is truly necessary. Limiting data sharing reduces exposure while improving privacy. Over time, these small decisions can significantly affect the amount of personal information available to third parties.

Privacy should not be viewed as a burden or obstacle. Rather, it should be seen as a form of personal responsibility similar to locking doors, safeguarding financial information, maintaining physical health, or protecting valuable possessions. Most privacy practices require only modest effort once established as habits. The benefits often far outweigh the time invested.

The ultimate objective of a privacy action plan is creating sustainable behaviors that support long-term security. Temporary efforts may provide short-term benefits, but lasting protection comes from routines that become integrated into everyday life. By combining appropriate technologies with informed habits, users can significantly reduce risk while maintaining the convenience and flexibility that mobile technology provides.

As you conclude this book, remember that privacy is a journey rather than a destination. New technologies, services, threats, and opportunities will continue emerging. The principles discussed throughout this book—awareness, preparation, encryption, secure communication, authentication, data minimization, and continuous learning—provide a foundation capable of adapting to future challenges. By applying these principles consistently, you can build a safer, more private, and more secure digital life for years to come.

Olivia discovered an important insight

Olivia had always enjoyed technology. Her smartphone connected her to friends, family, work, entertainment, education, and countless online services. Like most people, she appreciated the convenience of modern technology but rarely considered the privacy implications associated with daily digital activities.

That changed after a close friend became the victim of identity theft.

The experience was devastating. Unauthorized accounts were opened, financial records required correction, and months were spent recovering from the incident. Watching her friend navigate the aftermath made Olivia realize how vulnerable personal information could be.

Determined to improve her own security, Olivia began studying mobile privacy and cybersecurity. What started as simple curiosity gradually evolved into a comprehensive effort to strengthen her digital habits. She learned about encryption, VPNs, secure messaging, password management, multi-factor authentication, privacy settings, and data protection strategies.

Initially, the amount of information felt overwhelming.

"There must be a simpler way," she thought.

Eventually, Olivia discovered an important insight. Effective privacy did not require mastering every technical detail. Instead, it required building consistent habits that supported security goals. Rather than trying to solve everything at once, she focused on creating a practical action plan.

Her first step involved reviewing all of her online accounts.

The process took longer than expected. Over the years, she had accumulated accounts for shopping websites, streaming services, social media platforms, travel programs, educational resources, productivity tools, and various mobile applications. Some accounts had not been used in years.

As she reviewed each account, Olivia updated passwords, enabled multi-factor authentication, and closed services she no longer needed. By the end of the process, her digital footprint was significantly smaller and easier to manage.

Next, she focused on her smartphone.

Unused applications were removed. Permissions were reviewed. Privacy settings were adjusted. Software updates were installed. Device encryption was verified. Backup systems were tested. Each improvement strengthened her overall security posture.

Several months later, Olivia attended a community workshop on digital literacy. During a discussion session, participants shared their concerns about online privacy.

Some worried about social media tracking.

Others feared phishing attacks.

Many felt confused by the growing complexity of technology.

Olivia recognized those feelings because she had experienced them herself. Rather than offering complicated technical explanations, she described the practical habits that had helped her most.

"Start small," she advised.

"Protect your important accounts first. Use unique passwords. Turn on multi-factor authentication. Review app permissions. Keep your device updated. Build one habit at a time."

The advice resonated with many attendees because it felt achievable.

One participant named Robert approached her afterward. He admitted that cybersecurity often seemed intimidating because experts frequently discussed advanced concepts without addressing everyday realities.

Olivia explained that privacy was similar to physical fitness. People do not become healthy through a single workout. They develop health through consistent habits practiced over time. Privacy worked the same way.

Months later, Olivia received an email from Robert.

He explained that he had followed her advice and gradually implemented numerous improvements. He now used a password manager, enabled multi-factor authentication, reviewed privacy settings regularly, and educated his family about online safety.

Most importantly, he felt more confident.

That word stood out to Olivia.

Confidence.

She realized that confidence was one of the greatest benefits of a strong privacy strategy. Technology no longer felt mysterious or threatening. Instead, it became something she understood and managed intentionally.

Years passed.

Technology continued evolving. New devices appeared. Applications changed. Privacy regulations shifted.

Cybercriminals developed new tactics. Artificial intelligence transformed many aspects of digital life.

Yet Olivia's core habits remained effective.

She reviewed accounts regularly.

She protected important information.

She maintained backups.

She remained cautious when sharing data.

She stayed informed about emerging threats.

She treated privacy as an ongoing responsibility rather than a one-time project.

One evening, while helping her teenage nephew configure his first smartphone, Olivia reflected on how much she had learned. She taught him about passwords, authentication, secure browsing, privacy settings, and critical thinking.

More importantly, she taught him a mindset.

Technology should be used confidently, not fearfully.

Privacy should be managed intentionally, not ignored.

Security should be viewed as a habit, not an emergency response.

As her nephew listened attentively, Olivia realized that privacy education created lasting value. The tools and technologies might change, but the principles would remain relevant for decades.

Protect what matters.

Think before sharing.

Verify before trusting.

Stay informed.

Build good habits.

These principles had transformed her own digital life and could help others do the same.

Looking toward the future, Olivia felt optimistic. The digital world would undoubtedly continue presenting new challenges. Yet she knew that awareness, preparation, and consistent action provided a strong foundation for navigating those challenges successfully.

Her journey demonstrated a simple but powerful truth. Mobile privacy is not about achieving perfection or eliminating every risk. It is about making thoughtful choices, building sustainable habits, and maintaining control over the information that shapes our lives.

With knowledge, discipline, and the right tools, anyone can create a safer digital future. And that future begins with the small decisions made every day.

Chapter 8

The Future of Mobile Privacy, Emerging Threats, and Staying Secure in an AI-Driven World

Mobile technology continues to evolve at an extraordinary pace. Smartphones today possess computing power that exceeds that of many desktop computers from only a decade ago. They serve as communication hubs, financial management tools, health monitors, navigation systems, entertainment centers, business platforms, digital wallets, authentication devices, and personal assistants. As mobile technology becomes increasingly integrated into daily life, privacy and security challenges continue to evolve alongside it. Understanding future trends and emerging threats is essential for building a privacy strategy that remains effective over the long term.

One of the most significant developments affecting mobile privacy is the rapid growth of artificial intelligence. AI systems now influence search engines, social media platforms, recommendation systems, advertising networks, customer service tools, cybersecurity platforms, and mobile applications. While AI can improve convenience and efficiency, it also creates new opportunities for data collection, behavioral analysis, and user profiling. Mobile users must understand how AI systems operate and how their personal information may be used to train, improve, or power these technologies.

Modern AI systems rely heavily on data. Every interaction, search query, location history, purchasing behavior, communication pattern, and application preference may contribute to digital profiles used for personalization and analysis. While many AI-powered services provide valuable benefits, users should review privacy policies carefully and understand what information is being collected. Transparency, informed consent, and responsible data handling will become increasingly important as AI adoption expands.

Another emerging challenge involves predictive analytics. Predictive systems use large datasets and machine learning algorithms to forecast future behavior. These systems may estimate purchasing interests, financial preferences, health concerns, travel habits, political interests, or consumer decisions. While predictive analytics can improve user experiences, they also raise important privacy questions regarding data ownership, consent, and behavioral monitoring.

Mobile devices generate vast quantities of data that fuel predictive systems. Location information, browsing histories, application usage patterns, communication behaviors, and purchase records contribute to increasingly detailed user profiles. Privacy-conscious individuals should understand that information collected today may be analyzed in new ways tomorrow as technologies become more sophisticated.

Biometric authentication represents another area experiencing rapid growth. Smartphones increasingly rely on fingerprints, facial recognition systems, voice authentication, iris scanning, and behavioral biometrics to verify identity. Biometric systems offer convenience and often improve security compared to traditional passwords. However, biometric data is uniquely sensitive because it is permanently associated with an individual.

Unlike passwords, biometric characteristics cannot easily be changed if compromised. For this reason, users should ensure that biometric information is stored securely and processed using reputable security standards. Device manufacturers continue improving biometric protections, but users should remain informed about how these systems operate and what privacy safeguards are in place.

The Internet of Things, commonly referred to as IoT, further expands privacy considerations. Smartphones increasingly interact with smart home devices, wearable fitness trackers, smart vehicles, voice assistants, security cameras, connected appliances, and other internet-enabled technologies. Each connected device potentially generates additional data and introduces new security considerations.

A privacy-focused approach to IoT requires evaluating device security practices, software update policies, data collection methods, and vendor reputation. Users should understand what information connected devices collect, where that information is stored, and how it is shared. As the number of connected devices continues growing, managing privacy across an interconnected ecosystem becomes increasingly important.

Deepfake technology presents another emerging challenge. Advances in artificial intelligence now allow the creation of highly realistic synthetic images, videos, and audio recordings. While some applications are legitimate and creative, malicious actors may use deepfakes to impersonate individuals, spread misinformation, commit fraud, or manipulate public perception.

Mobile users should develop healthy skepticism when evaluating digital content. Verification of sources, confirmation through multiple channels, and critical thinking skills become increasingly important as synthetic media grows more sophisticated. Trust should be earned through verification rather than assumed based solely on appearance.

Cybercriminals are also adopting artificial intelligence to improve attack effectiveness. AI-powered phishing campaigns can generate highly personalized messages based on publicly available information. Automated systems may analyze social media activity, professional profiles, and online behavior to craft convincing scams. These attacks often appear more legitimate than traditional phishing attempts and may be harder to identify.

Defending against AI-enhanced attacks requires strong fundamentals. Users should verify requests independently, avoid responding to unexpected messages, scrutinize links carefully, and remain cautious when sharing sensitive information. While attack methods evolve, many successful scams continue relying on human trust and emotional manipulation rather than technical sophistication.

Cloud computing will continue playing a major role in mobile technology. Increasing amounts of personal information are stored remotely rather than directly on devices. Cloud services provide convenience, synchronization, collaboration, and backup capabilities. However, they also concentrate large amounts of data within centralized systems. Users should evaluate cloud providers based on encryption practices, privacy policies, authentication controls, transparency, and security history.

Quantum computing represents a future technology that may eventually affect modern encryption systems. While practical quantum threats remain limited at present, researchers are actively developing quantum-resistant cryptographic algorithms designed to protect future communications. Security professionals, governments, and technology companies are preparing for eventual transitions to stronger encryption standards capable of resisting quantum attacks.

Digital identity management will likely become increasingly important. Smartphones already function as authentication devices for banking, government services, healthcare systems, business platforms, and online accounts. Future digital identity systems may include additional verification mechanisms, digital credentials, and secure identity frameworks designed to reduce fraud while protecting privacy.

Privacy regulations are also evolving globally. Governments around the world continue developing laws that address data collection, consumer rights, consent requirements, transparency obligations, and cybersecurity standards. Understanding applicable privacy rights can help users make informed decisions about how their information is collected, stored, and shared.

Data ownership remains a central topic in privacy discussions. Many individuals are becoming more aware of the value associated with personal information. Questions regarding who owns data, who controls access, and how information can be used will likely remain important for years to come. Users who understand these issues can make more informed decisions about the services they use and the information they choose to share.

Despite the complexity of emerging technologies, several privacy principles remain remarkably stable. Strong authentication, encryption, secure communication, responsible data sharing, software updates, careful application selection, and user education continue providing effective protection. While tools and threats may change, these foundational principles remain relevant across technological generations.

Adaptability is perhaps the most important long-term security skill. Technology evolves rapidly, and users who remain curious, informed, and flexible are better positioned to respond to new challenges. Continuous learning allows individuals to evaluate emerging technologies critically and adopt beneficial innovations without compromising privacy unnecessarily.

It is also important to maintain perspective. News headlines often emphasize worst-case scenarios, creating unnecessary fear. While genuine risks exist, modern technology also offers tremendous opportunities for education, communication, creativity, healthcare, business growth, and personal development. Effective privacy strategies seek balance rather than isolation. The goal is to enjoy technological benefits while minimizing unnecessary risks.

Ultimately, the future of mobile privacy will depend not only on technology companies, governments, and cybersecurity professionals but also on individual users. Informed decisions, responsible habits, and thoughtful use of privacy tools empower individuals to maintain greater control over their digital lives. By combining strong security practices with ongoing education, users can navigate an increasingly complex digital landscape with confidence.

As you complete this book, remember that privacy is not a destination reached once and permanently secured. It is a continuing process of awareness, adaptation, and responsible decision-making. The tools discussed throughout this book provide a strong foundation, but the most powerful privacy asset remains an informed and engaged user who understands both the opportunities and risks of the digital world.

Ethan had focused primarily on traditional cybersecurity concerns

Ethan sat at a coffee shop watching people around him interact with technology. Some were using smartphones to conduct business meetings. Others communicated through video calls, managed investments, streamed entertainment, or controlled smart home devices remotely. Technology had become deeply woven into daily life.

As a technology consultant, Ethan spent years helping businesses implement digital systems. He appreciated innovation and recognized the tremendous opportunities created by modern technology. At the same time, he understood that every technological advancement introduced new privacy and security considerations.

Several years earlier, Ethan had focused primarily on traditional cybersecurity concerns such as malware, phishing attacks, password management, and network security. Recently, however, new challenges had begun attracting attention.

Artificial intelligence.

Deepfakes.

Predictive analytics.

Advanced surveillance technologies.

Connected ecosystems.

These developments fascinated him because they represented the future of digital life.

One afternoon, Ethan attended a technology conference featuring experts in artificial intelligence, cybersecurity, and privacy law. During one presentation, a researcher demonstrated how AI systems could analyze vast amounts of public information to generate highly detailed behavioral profiles.

The demonstration was impressive but also unsettling.

Within minutes, the system identified likely interests, purchasing patterns, travel preferences, and communication habits based on publicly available information. The presentation highlighted both the power and potential risks associated with large-scale data analysis.

Afterward, Ethan discussed the topic with a privacy researcher named Maya.

"The technology isn't inherently good or bad," Maya explained. "The real question is how it's used and whether people understand what's happening with their data."

That conversation stayed with Ethan long after the conference ended.

Determined to better understand emerging privacy challenges, he began studying AI-powered applications, connected devices, and data collection practices. He examined how smartphones interacted with cloud services, wearable devices, smart assistants, and social platforms.

The deeper he looked, the clearer a pattern became.

Technology was becoming more interconnected every year.

Information flowed continuously between devices, services, and platforms. Convenience increased dramatically, but so did opportunities for data collection.

Rather than rejecting technology, Ethan focused on developing practical strategies for maintaining privacy within this evolving environment. He reviewed application permissions carefully, evaluated privacy policies, strengthened authentication systems, and remained selective about the services he used.

One day, a colleague named Jessica approached him with a concern.

She had recently seen a video online that appeared to show a well-known public figure making controversial statements. Later, news organizations revealed that the video was an AI-generated deepfake.

Jessica was shocked.

"If videos can be faked this convincingly, how do we know what to trust anymore?" she asked.

Ethan explained that verification would become increasingly important. As synthetic media improved, people would need to rely on multiple sources, corroborating evidence, and critical thinking rather than accepting content at face value.

Their conversation highlighted a broader reality.

The future of privacy and security would depend not only on technology but also on human judgment.

Over the following years, Ethan incorporated this lesson into his professional work. When advising clients, he emphasized adaptability rather than specific tools. Technologies would change. Platforms would evolve. Threats would emerge and disappear.

However, certain principles remained consistent.

Verify information.

Protect sensitive data.

Use strong authentication.

Limit unnecessary exposure.

Stay informed.

Think critically.

These principles formed the foundation of digital resilience.

One evening, Ethan visited his parents and noticed how much technology had changed their lives. Smart speakers controlled lighting systems. Health-monitoring devices tracked fitness metrics. Smartphones managed finances, appointments, transportation, and communication.

The conveniences were undeniable.

Yet Ethan also recognized the importance of helping family members understand privacy implications associated with connected devices.

During dinner, they discussed practical steps for improving security. His parents learned how to review permissions, enable authentication features, update software, and evaluate privacy settings. The conversation focused on empowerment rather than fear.

Years later, Ethan looked back on the rapid technological changes he had witnessed. Smartphones had become more powerful. Artificial intelligence had become more capable. Connected devices had become more common. Privacy debates had become more complex.

Despite these changes, one lesson remained remarkably clear.

Technology itself was only part of the equation.

The most important factor was the individual using it.

Informed users could make thoughtful decisions.

Educated users could adapt to new threats.

Prepared users could benefit from innovation while maintaining control over personal information.

As Ethan watched the next generation embrace emerging technologies, he felt optimistic. Challenges would undoubtedly arise, but opportunities would as well. Privacy and innovation did not need to exist in conflict. With awareness, responsibility, and continuous learning, both could coexist.

Standing outside beneath the evening sky, Ethan reflected on the future.

No one could predict every technological development that lay ahead. New inventions would emerge. New threats would appear. New opportunities would transform society.

But one thing remained certain.

The individuals best prepared for that future would not necessarily be those with the most advanced technology. They would be those who understood how technology worked, valued their privacy, adapted to change, and took responsibility for protecting their digital lives.

And that understanding would remain one of the most powerful security tools of all.

Chapter 9

Mobile Privacy Mastery – Real-World Scenarios, Crisis Response, and Protecting Yourself When Things Go Wrong

One of the most important realities of cybersecurity is that no system is perfect. Even users who follow best practices, use strong passwords, enable multi-factor authentication, utilize VPNs, encrypt communications, and carefully manage privacy settings may eventually encounter security incidents. Devices can be lost. Accounts can be targeted. Scams can succeed. New vulnerabilities can emerge. The true measure of mobile privacy mastery is not whether problems ever occur but how effectively users respond when they do.

Many people spend considerable time learning prevention strategies but very little time preparing for incident response. As a result, when problems arise, panic often replaces rational decision-making. Panic can lead to mistakes, delays, poor choices, and increased damage. Developing a response plan before an incident occurs helps users remain calm and take appropriate action when faced with unexpected challenges.

One of the most common mobile security incidents involves device loss or theft. Smartphones contain enormous amounts of personal and professional information. If a device is misplaced, stolen, or left unattended, users should act quickly. The first step is attempting to locate the device using built-in tracking features provided by the operating system. Most modern smartphones include tools that allow users to view device locations, trigger sounds, display messages, lock devices remotely, or erase data when recovery appears unlikely.

Preparation is critical. Remote management capabilities must be enabled before a device is lost. Users should verify these settings during routine security reviews. Device encryption should also be activated so that data remains protected even if attackers gain physical possession of the hardware. Strong authentication measures provide an additional layer of protection while users work to recover or secure lost devices.

Account compromise represents another frequent security challenge. Users may discover unfamiliar login notifications, suspicious account activity, unauthorized purchases, password reset messages, or altered account settings. When account compromise is suspected, immediate action is necessary. Users should change passwords, revoke active sessions, review account recovery settings, and verify multi-factor authentication configurations.

Email accounts deserve special attention because they often serve as recovery mechanisms for other services. If attackers gain access to a primary email account, they may attempt to reset passwords for banking platforms, social media accounts, cloud services, and business systems. Securing email accounts should therefore be a top priority during incident response efforts.

Phishing attacks continue to be among the most successful cybercrime techniques because they target human behavior rather than technical vulnerabilities. Attackers frequently impersonate banks, government agencies, employers, delivery services, social media platforms, and technology companies. Messages often create urgency, fear, excitement, or curiosity to encourage rapid action.

Recognizing phishing attacks requires attention to detail. Users should verify sender identities, examine domain names carefully, avoid clicking unexpected links, and independently confirm requests involving sensitive information. If a phishing attempt succeeds, users should immediately change affected passwords, review account activity, and monitor for signs of additional compromise.

Malware infections present another potential crisis scenario. Symptoms may include unusual battery drain, excessive data usage, unauthorized advertisements, unexplained application behavior, device slowdowns, unexpected permissions requests, or suspicious network activity. If malware is suspected, users should disconnect from untrusted networks, remove suspicious applications, update security software, and consider professional assistance if necessary.

Data breaches have become increasingly common. Organizations of all sizes may experience incidents exposing customer information. When notified of a breach, users should determine what information was affected and assess potential risks. Compromised credentials should be changed immediately, especially if passwords were reused elsewhere. Monitoring financial accounts, credit reports, and identity-related information may also be appropriate depending on the nature of the breach.

Identity theft remains one of the most damaging consequences of privacy failures. Criminals may use stolen information to open accounts, apply for loans, file fraudulent tax returns, obtain medical services, or conduct financial transactions. Early detection is critical. Users should monitor financial statements, account notifications, credit reports, and authentication alerts for signs of suspicious activity.

Mobile payment fraud continues growing as digital wallets and contactless payment systems become more popular. Users should review transactions regularly, enable transaction notifications, and report unauthorized activity immediately. Financial institutions often provide fraud protection programs, but prompt reporting significantly improves recovery outcomes.

Social media incidents can also create privacy challenges. Account takeovers, impersonation attempts, unauthorized posts, data scraping, and reputation attacks may affect users personally and professionally. Strong authentication, privacy settings, and cautious sharing practices help reduce these risks. If incidents occur, users should report unauthorized activity quickly and document relevant evidence.

One often overlooked aspect of crisis response is evidence preservation. During security incidents, users may be tempted to delete messages, erase logs, or remove files immediately. While removing threats is important, preserving evidence can assist investigations, support recovery efforts, and provide valuable information for security professionals. Screenshots, email headers, account notifications, and transaction records may prove useful later.

Communication management is another important consideration. During significant incidents, users should communicate through trusted channels rather than relying on potentially compromised systems. If email accounts are affected, alternative communication methods may be necessary. Family members, employers, financial institutions, and service providers may need to be informed depending on the circumstances.

Psychological factors often influence incident response. Cybersecurity incidents can create stress, embarrassment, frustration, and anxiety. Many victims blame themselves even when sophisticated attackers are involved. Maintaining perspective is important. Cybercriminals succeed because they exploit human behavior and continuously refine their methods. Learning from incidents is more productive than dwelling on mistakes.

Developing a personal incident response checklist can significantly improve preparedness. Such a checklist may include emergency contact information, account recovery procedures, backup verification steps, device tracking instructions, financial institution contact details, and documentation requirements. Having a predefined plan reduces uncertainty during stressful situations.

Privacy-conscious users should also prepare for worst-case scenarios. This does not mean expecting disaster but rather ensuring resilience. Backups should exist. Recovery methods should be tested. Important documents should be stored securely. Authentication recovery options should be verified. These preparations allow users to recover more quickly if serious incidents occur.

Another valuable practice involves conducting simulated scenarios. Just as organizations perform emergency drills, individuals can mentally rehearse responses to potential incidents. What would you do if your smartphone disappeared today? What steps would you take if your primary email account were compromised? How would you recover access if you lost authentication devices? Thinking through these situations in advance improves readiness.

The concept of resilience remains central to privacy mastery. Security incidents are often viewed as failures, but resilience focuses on recovery and adaptation. Resilient users anticipate challenges, prepare accordingly, and maintain the ability to recover from setbacks. This mindset transforms cybersecurity from a source of fear into a manageable aspect of modern life.

Technology will continue evolving, and new threats will emerge. Yet many response principles remain constant. Stay calm. Assess the situation. Secure affected systems. Preserve evidence. Communicate appropriately. Learn from the experience. Improve protections moving forward. These principles apply across a wide range of privacy and security incidents.

Ultimately, mobile privacy mastery involves more than preventing problems. It involves developing the confidence and capability to respond effectively when problems occur. By preparing in advance, maintaining strong habits, and understanding recovery processes, users can significantly reduce the impact of security incidents and protect what matters most.

Marcus considered himself reasonably prepared for digital threats.

Over the years, he had learned about strong passwords, multi-factor authentication, VPNs, encrypted communications, and privacy-focused applications. He regularly updated his smartphone, reviewed permissions, and maintained secure backups.

Despite these precautions, he never expected to experience a major security incident himself.

That assumption changed during a business trip.

After a long day of meetings, Marcus stopped at a busy restaurant before returning to his hotel. While paying for dinner, he briefly placed his smartphone on the table. Moments later, it was gone.

At first, he assumed he had misplaced it.

He searched the restaurant, checked his pockets, retraced his steps, and asked employees for assistance. The phone remained missing.

A wave of anxiety immediately followed.

His smartphone contained years of personal information, business communications, financial applications, family photographs, and authentication tools. Losing the device felt like losing a piece of his life.

Then he remembered something important.

Preparation.

Months earlier, Marcus had enabled device tracking, remote management features, encryption, and secure backups. Instead of panicking, he borrowed a colleague's device and logged into his account management portal.

Within minutes, he located the phone.

The tracking system showed movement away from the restaurant. Recovery appeared unlikely.

Marcus remotely locked the device, displayed a contact message, and monitored its location. When movement continued, he initiated a remote wipe to protect sensitive information.

Although disappointed, he felt relieved knowing that the data remained protected.

The following morning introduced a second challenge.

While reviewing account notifications, Marcus noticed several unusual login attempts targeting one of his email accounts. Whether related to the stolen phone or simply a coincidence, he could not be certain.

Again, preparation proved valuable.

Strong passwords, multi-factor authentication, and account monitoring prevented unauthorized access. Marcus changed credentials, reviewed account activity, verified recovery settings, and notified relevant service providers.

The incidents served as a powerful reminder that security events rarely occur according to convenient schedules.

Upon returning home, Marcus decided to conduct a comprehensive review of his privacy strategy.

He updated his incident response checklist.

Emergency contacts were organized.

Recovery procedures were documented.

Authentication backup methods were verified.

Important account information was stored securely.

The process strengthened his confidence because he now had a clear plan for future incidents.

Several months later, Marcus received an alarming email appearing to originate from his bank. The message warned of suspicious activity and instructed him to verify account information immediately.

The email looked convincing.

Logos appeared authentic.

Formatting matched previous communications.

The language sounded professional.

Years earlier, Marcus might have responded without hesitation.

Instead, he paused.

Carefully examining the message, he noticed subtle inconsistencies in the sender address. Rather than clicking the provided link, he opened his banking application directly and contacted customer support through official channels.

The email was fraudulent.

Because of his training and experience, he recognized the deception before any damage occurred.

Later that year, Marcus joined a community cybersecurity awareness program. During one workshop, participants shared stories about digital challenges they had encountered.

Some described phishing attacks.

Others discussed identity theft.

Several reported social media compromises.

Many admitted feeling overwhelmed when incidents occurred.

Marcus shared his own experience with the stolen smartphone.

However, rather than focusing on the theft itself, he emphasized the importance of preparation.

"The device wasn't what saved me," he explained.

"The preparation saved me."

Tracking features, encryption, backups, authentication controls, and recovery plans transformed a potentially devastating incident into a manageable inconvenience.

His story resonated with the audience because it demonstrated a practical truth.

Security is not about avoiding every possible problem.

It is about being prepared when problems occur.

Over time, Marcus became known among friends and colleagues as someone who approached technology thoughtfully. People often sought his advice after encountering suspicious messages or privacy concerns.

His recommendations remained remarkably consistent.

Use strong passwords.

Enable multi-factor authentication.

Maintain backups.

Review permissions.

Prepare recovery plans.

Stay calm during incidents.

Learn from experience.

These principles were not complicated, yet they proved extraordinarily effective.

Years later, Marcus reflected on how his perspective had evolved.

Initially, he viewed cybersecurity primarily as a technical challenge involving software, devices, and tools. Eventually, he realized that resilience was equally important.

Resilience meant preparing for uncertainty.

Resilience meant recovering from setbacks.

Resilience meant adapting and improving after incidents occurred.

Most importantly, resilience meant maintaining confidence despite an ever-changing threat landscape.

As technology continued advancing, Marcus knew new risks would emerge. New attack methods would appear. New devices would enter the market. New privacy concerns would capture headlines.

Yet he also understood that preparation, awareness, and adaptability would remain valuable regardless of technological changes.

The future would undoubtedly bring challenges.

But it would also bring opportunities for those willing to learn, prepare, and take responsibility for protecting their digital lives.

Standing outside one evening, looking at the city lights illuminated by countless connected devices, Marcus smiled.

He no longer feared technology.

He respected it.

And through preparation, knowledge, and resilience, he felt ready for whatever came next.

Final Thoughts: Protecting Your Freedom, Privacy, and Future in a Connected World

The smartphone has become one of the most powerful tools ever created. It allows people to communicate instantly across continents, manage businesses from virtually anywhere, access unlimited information, control finances, navigate unfamiliar locations, capture memories, learn new skills, and maintain relationships with friends, family members, clients, and colleagues. What once required multiple devices and significant resources can now be accomplished from a single device that fits comfortably in a pocket. Yet with this extraordinary convenience comes responsibility. Throughout this book, you have learned that privacy and security are no longer optional considerations. They are essential life skills for anyone living in a digitally connected world.

Many people assume that cybersecurity is only relevant to large corporations, government agencies, technology professionals, or wealthy individuals. The truth is that every smartphone user possesses information that has value. Personal photographs, financial records, private conversations, location histories, login credentials, health information, business communications, and digital identities all represent assets that deserve protection. Cybercriminals do not always target people because they are wealthy or famous. Often, they target individuals simply because opportunities exist. Understanding this reality is the first step toward building a safer digital life.

One of the most important lessons throughout this book is that privacy is not about secrecy. Privacy is about control. It is about deciding who has access to your information, when that access occurs, and how your data is used. Most people are not trying to hide anything. Instead, they seek reasonable protections for their personal lives, families, businesses, finances, and communications. Just as people lock their homes, protect their vehicles, and secure important documents, they should also take reasonable measures to protect their digital information.

VPNs represent one of the most valuable tools available for improving mobile privacy. By encrypting internet traffic and creating secure connections between devices and remote servers, VPNs help reduce exposure to network monitoring and improve protection on public Wi-Fi networks. Throughout this book, you have learned that VPNs are not magical solutions that eliminate all risks. Rather, they serve as one important layer within a larger privacy strategy. When used correctly, VPNs provide meaningful protection while allowing users to maintain flexibility and convenience.

Encryption serves as the foundation of modern digital security. Whether protecting messages, financial transactions, cloud storage, backups, websites, or mobile applications, encryption helps ensure that sensitive information remains accessible only to authorized parties. Most users interact with encryption every day without realizing it. Understanding how encryption works allows individuals to appreciate its value and make informed decisions about which services and tools deserve their trust.

Secure browsing practices remain equally important. Every online interaction creates opportunities for both convenience and risk. Websites, advertising networks, analytics platforms, data brokers, and malicious actors may all attempt to collect information about users. By choosing secure browsers, using privacy-focused search tools, verifying website authenticity, enabling tracking protections, and remaining cautious when sharing information, users can significantly reduce unnecessary exposure while enjoying the benefits of the modern internet.

The rise of artificial intelligence, predictive analytics, connected devices, biometric systems, and cloud-based services will continue transforming the digital landscape. New opportunities will emerge alongside new privacy challenges. While technology evolves rapidly, the principles discussed throughout this book remain remarkably consistent. Strong authentication, encryption, responsible data sharing, regular software updates, secure communications, privacy awareness, and continuous learning will continue providing effective protection regardless of future technological developments.

Perhaps the most valuable lesson is that cybersecurity is ultimately about habits rather than technology. The most advanced security tools cannot fully protect users who ignore warnings, reuse passwords, disable security features, or share sensitive information carelessly. Conversely, individuals who develop strong habits often achieve impressive levels of protection even without extensive technical expertise. Small actions performed consistently over time create meaningful improvements in privacy and security.

The concept of defense in depth has appeared repeatedly throughout this book because it represents one of the most effective approaches to cybersecurity. Rather than relying on a single tool or technique, users should build multiple layers of protection. Strong passwords protect accounts. Multi-factor authentication adds verification. Encryption protects data. VPNs secure internet traffic. Secure browsers reduce tracking.

Backups ensure recoverability. Together, these layers create a resilient system capable of withstanding many common threats.

It is also important to recognize that mistakes happen. Devices may be lost. Accounts may be compromised. Phishing attacks may succeed. New vulnerabilities may emerge. Perfection is not the goal. Resilience is the goal. Users who prepare for potential incidents, maintain backups, verify recovery options, and understand response procedures can recover more quickly when challenges occur. Resilience transforms cybersecurity from a source of fear into a manageable aspect of modern life.

Families play an important role in digital privacy. Children, teenagers, parents, and grandparents all face unique challenges when using technology. Sharing knowledge, discussing risks openly, and establishing healthy digital habits create stronger protection for everyone. Privacy education should not be limited to technical professionals. It should become part of everyday conversations, much like discussions about physical safety, financial responsibility, and personal well-being.

Business owners, entrepreneurs, remote workers, students, travelers, and everyday users all benefit from understanding privacy principles. Regardless of profession or lifestyle, smartphones have become gateways to information, opportunities, and relationships. Protecting these devices means protecting the systems and people connected to them. Every security improvement contributes to a safer digital environment for individuals, families, organizations, and communities.

As technology continues evolving, it is easy to become overwhelmed by headlines discussing cybercrime, surveillance, data breaches, artificial intelligence, and privacy concerns. While these issues deserve attention, they should not create fear. Instead, they should encourage awareness. The goal is not to disconnect from technology but to use it intelligently. Informed users can embrace innovation while maintaining control over their information and reducing unnecessary risks.

Throughout this book, you have gained the knowledge necessary to build a comprehensive mobile privacy strategy. You understand how VPNs function, how encryption protects communications, how tracking systems operate, how privacy-focused tools reduce exposure, how to secure accounts, how to respond to incidents, and how to adapt to emerging technologies. More importantly, you understand the mindset required for long-term success. Privacy is not a destination. It is an ongoing process of learning, adapting, and making informed choices.

The future will undoubtedly bring new devices, new applications, new services, and new challenges. However, the principles discussed throughout these pages will remain valuable. Awareness, preparation, responsibility, and continuous improvement provide a strong foundation for navigating an increasingly connected world. By applying these principles consistently, you can protect your personal information, support your goals, safeguard your family, and enjoy the benefits of technology with greater confidence.

As you finish this book, remember that the most powerful privacy tool is not a VPN, encryption algorithm, browser, or application. The most powerful privacy tool is an informed user who understands how technology works and takes responsibility for protecting what matters most. Knowledge creates awareness. Awareness drives action. Action builds security. Security creates confidence.

May the lessons contained in this book help you build a safer digital future, strengthen your mobile privacy, and navigate the connected world with wisdom, confidence, and control.

www.ingramcontent.com/pod-product-compliance
Lightning Source LLC
LaVergne TN
LVHW030726061126
851857LV00019B/2015

* 9 7 9 8 2 4 0 8 1 5 0 8 9 *